Brilliant account of a real woman's struggle to fight through death, depression, anger, and abuse and still take control of her destiny. Thank you, Lynette, for showing us how to live.

—JULIAN LARK
EDITOR-IN-CHIEF, *KONTROL* MAGAZINE

Truly an inspirational book, by one of God's great and humble servants. Lynette shows us how to fight for and through life with God on your side. A must read for anyone struggling with the pain of addictions.

—DAN DARLING
CHIEF INFORMATION OFFICER, TURNER BROADCASTING SYSTEMS

Lynette takes us on her real, transparent, life-changing journey. Her heartfelt words, struggles, fears and ultimate triumph encourage us all to never give up, cave in, or quit!

—JENNIFER KITT
CHIEF EMPOWERMENT OFFICER,
TODAY'S BLACK WOMAN'S RADIO SHOW,
KISS 104.1

I stand in awe of Lynette's honesty, determination, courage, and wisdom through her journey in *Hollow*. In this book she shows us that we don't always get to choose what happens to us in life; but we can choose how we deal with life's challenges. Everything we need is inside us and Lynette shows us that with God on your side, nothing is impossible.

Many themes run through this story. One such theme is the power of God's love in the thick of crisis and loss. *Hollow* is a compassionate, spiritual offering that candidly shares the power of God's redemptive love. It will make you cry. It will have you laughing. By the end of this read you will want to live and love again. Thank you, Lynette, for your translucency and willingness to share *Hollow* with us.

—DR. HART RAMSEY
SENIOR PASTOR OF NORTHVIEW CHRISTIAN CHURCH
DOTHAN, ALABAMA

HOLLOW

WHEN EVERYTHING THAT MEANS ANYTHING IS TAKEN AWAY

LYNETTE JACKSON

HOLLOW by Lynette Jackson
Published by Creation House Press (CHP)
A Charisma Media Company
600 Rinehart Road
Lake Mary, Florida 32746
www.charismamedia.com

Unless otherwise noted, all Scripture quotations are from the King James Version of the Holy Bible.

Design Director: Bill Johnson
Cover design by Terry Clifton

Visit the author's website: www.Lynette.TV

Library of Congress Cataloging-in-Publication Data: 2013937676
International Standard Book Number: 978-1-62136-386-6

While the author has made every effort to provide accurate telephone numbers and Internet addresses at the time of publication, neither the publisher nor the author assumes any responsibility for errors or for changes that occur after publication.

First edition

13 14 15 16 17 — 9 8 7 6 5 4 3 2 1
Printed in the United States of America

Dedication

I joyfully dedicate this book to:

Christine White

Mom, there is not a day that goes by that I don't long to hear your voice and feel the comfort of your touch. You have taught me to be strong and to value life, even while you were facing death. Each day when I look at my hands I see you. These are the same hands that have wiped many tears, consoled many friends, and embraced the unembraceable.

You have shown me how to mother my children and grandmother my grandson. "Unless a corn of wheat fall into the ground and die, it abideth alone: but if it die, it bringeth forth much fruit" (John 12:24). I am that fruit; thanks for being the seed.

Walter and Shardie Williams

Walter, you have always been my quiet voice of reason and the voice that talks me out of trees. You have given me two of the greatest gifts a mother could ask for: a beautiful daughter, Shardie Williams, and my first grandchild, Christopher Anthony Williams. You are an amazing protector and provider. When I watch you with your son I see the love that God has for his children shown through you. Shardie, I don't consider you my daughter-in-law, you are my daughter. I love you, girl, don't make me cry.

Ronald Jackson

My baby boy, before you were born I knew you had the makings of greatness. You have taught me how to laugh even when I felt like crying. You changed my vision about music, poetry, and philosophy. You showed me how to be open to new ideas, creations, and concepts. I love the revelation that speaks through you. Thanks for keeping it real and sharing your mind.

To My Family

Words alone are not enough to express what you mean to me. When I look at our family I see a tree, strong at the roots with a firm foundation—the trunk standing steadfast and unmovable. From the trunk are the branches, which represent our individuality—some small, some large. But through all the storms we have weathered together, we still stand strong. I love you!

Furnice White, Alma White, and George Quarles

You left too soon, but your memories remain forever.

CONTENTS

CONTENTS

Acknowledgments

To almighty God, who is the author and finisher of my life and faith. Thank you for changing how I see your creation. Now I can clearly see the path that has been planned for me. Thank you for showing me your unconditional love even when I felt unlovable.

Dan Darling, CIO, Turner Broadcasting—A true man of wisdom, knowledge, and understanding. Although I don't work for you anymore, you are still the boss. You have taught me leadership that breaks barriers.

Jim Walton, former president of CNN News Group—I will never forget the day you told me that I was no longer on my own life list. You opened my eyes and revealed to me that not only should I be on my list, but I should be at the top of it.

Jim Consuegra, Scuba Master—You told me on my first night in scuba class when I asked you a million question about sharks that one day I would not only pay to see them but I was going to go out of my way to see one. As usual, you were right. Thanks for teaching me how to trust again.

Orlando Gladney—I can't express my gratitude enough for sharing your eating plan with me even though I got mad at you for throwing my cheese eggs in the trash. I forgive you, and I thank you!

Paul Campbell—Thanks for always encouraging me to keep my head down while swimming and teaching me to roll with the current. I always feel safe when diving with you!

Sherry Garrett—I would not have my scuba certification if it were not for you. Thank you for encouraging me to finish. God brings people into our life for a reason, and I am so glad I met you. You are truly a friend and buddy!

Antwan Mills, Personal Trainer—You had me when you pulled out the anatomy books and showed me how God designed our bodies to look and work. Thank you for teaching me how to breathe.

Pastor Bank and Sharon Akinmola—Thanks for always believing in me and showing me how big the God that lives on the inside of me is.

Pastor Harry and Kay Riley—Thank you for loving my mother. She truly loved you both, and I know she is still praying for you.

Sheronne Burke, BFF—God knew what He was doing when He introduced us. He knew I would need a BFF that would make me laugh, cry, and allow me to just be me. I love the fact that we don't have to say anything to know what each of us is thinking. How do you know a true friend? They show up. Thanks for showing up in every way!

Simone Walker, Editor—A book is only as good as its editor. Thank you so much for seeing my vision and helping me bring it to life. You are an amazing, powerful woman that God will use in a mighty way. Are you ready?

To all the Facebook and Twitter friends and family—Thanks for supporting my dreams and visions. I thank God for you.

There are so many people that I want to thank who have walked this journey with me. If I wrote something about each of you, I would have to publish a new book.

So I will just say a BIG THANK YOU to:

Annette Cloud Parker, Carol and Mike Peros, Cindy Meade Consuegra, Inez Savage, Assunto Banks, Phillip and Rosie Alequin, James Tate, Keith Dobbins, Veronica Sheehan, Lanel Shepherd, Tim Thomas, Jennifer Montgomery Holmes, Javis Brown, Sonnie Beverly, Jeff Bradshaw, Denise Armstrong, Shirleen Boone, Brittney Burke, Thom Murrell, Evelyn Mims, Chuck Lampman, Shea Gibson, Raynard Gibson, Rick Odom, DeEtta West, Patricia Daniels, Angela Latham Hickman, David Anderson Ruby Clarke Walker, Lindsey Esber, Sherrell Web, Hayes Fountain, Barbara Shaw, Gene Banks, Chaka Cox, Angela Jones, Vickie Hammond, Donzalia Simmons Rogers, Stephen James, Vincent McCant, Elijah Sterling, A.J. Belefonte, Lisa Fitch, Alverta Walker, Desiree Brown, Mario Jones, Tracy Escaravage Powers, Mackenzie Burke, Charles McCollough, Tifani Noles, Barbara Goodfellow, Yvonne Garner, Chef Dejoie, Shawn Brooks, Mark Mackey, Michelle Bowens, Robin Sillers, Ina Latham, Carla Bragg Harrison, Deneen Whatley, Debbie Brown, Kevin Smith, Vic Bolton, Pastor Jeff Taylor, Danny L Russ, Valeria and Kenneth Walker, Annette Craig, Chelsea Symone Burke, Jessie Nelson, MalaniKai VII, Nichole Serchion, Debora Denise Alexander, Sarah Mckenzie, Eunah Marie Francis, Tashan Parks Twyman, Ermina Hill, Steve Almasy, Anna Kovats, Vicky Raimey, Jeff Sparks, Alisa Deans, Carl Anthony, Cheryle Coleman Harrison, Lauriann Davies Stepp, Victor Hogan, Marty Holder, Tumaini Publishing, Kenny Rushing, Shaunn Wyche, Grace Carrington, Donnel Davis, Sherita Cherry Williams, Kenneth Haynes, Tommie Gardner, Trina Kat Dunan, Kevin Belcher, Deirdra Jackson Henderson, Larry

Live, Martin Williams, Bridgette Hunter, Steve Millen, Justin Hollywood, Jeff McGuire, Edith Quansah, Beth Webster, Yolanda Moody, Anthony White, and everyone whose name isn't listed here but played a critical role in my life during this journey. Thank you all.

PART I

THE HOLLOWING

Introduction

THE CHOCOLATE EASTER BUNNY

ACH YEAR AS a child I received a plastic Easter basket filled with goodies from my parents. In the center of that basket was always the biggest and most beautiful chocolate Easter bunny I had ever seen. This wonderful, tasty treat was the highlight of each Easter—even more so than the dresses and eggs and holiday festivities. However, the one thing that always bothered me about that Easter bunny was the fact that it was *hollow*.

I am the youngest of seven children—six girls and one boy. My father was a truck driver, and my mother was a homemaker. Limited to one income and many mouths to feed, sweets and candy were a luxury that we were only afforded on Easter and Christmas. On Easter, we were always assured of receiving that wonderful basket filled with delicious goodies.

Despite my love for that delicious chocolate bunny, I recall feeling cheated because the center was hollow, and, if you were not careful, the entire thing could crumble in your hands. Each year I savored this treat, and so I would carefully and strategically eat the ears, then the tail, and finally the feet. But once I got to the center—the core—it would inevitably crumble. At that time I would lose interest in my chocolate bunny because it had lost its beauty and it no longer appealed to my appetite.

Like my beloved chocolate bunny, a few years ago I recognized that I too had a hollow core; my beauty crumbled, and I lost my appetite for life. As a result of a series of life-altering circumstances, anger, denial, and depression consumed my core, leaving me with a hollow soul. I dealt with—or rather didn't deal with—my emotions with the help of food, alcohol, and prescription painkillers. During this period in my life I cried often and felt a deep sadness for loved ones who had left me. My refusal to deal with the tragedies in my life sent me on a treacherous downward spiral. Through it all I realized I neglected and abused the person who should have meant the most in my life—me!

I believe my hollowing began with divorce; deepened as I began dating; reached unfathomable depths with the death of my mother, nephew, and sister; and, as if that weren't enough, I lost my job and was betrayed by the church—all within a few short years. With each event I felt like someone was eating pieces of my life, like that chocolate Easter bunny, until they got to the center, the core, the very essence of my being. And when I crumbled they lost interest, leaving me abandoned, unloved, used, and abused.

As I write this book I am now fifty years old, single, and a mother of two handsome sons. Walter, thirty, is married with his own son, and Ronald, twenty, is a junior in college. It took me a while to realize that I had raised them from behind a mask. I was a master at the masquerade. You see, I was always putting on the smile, trying to lead a wonderful life as a Christian, naming it and claiming it, blabbing it and grabbing it, all the while suffering silently and too embarrassed to talk about it. I felt pretty on the outside at times but led a very lonely, scared life behind closed doors.

In my world I was always the positive one, the one who would give good advice to people, the one who had the answers; but no one had the answers for me. I was the one my friends and family would call on when they had a problem. But when

I had a problem they told me, "You're the strong one," "You can do it," or "You will be OK, girl. Just keep praying, standing, and believing." The reality was that I was hurting, broken, and lonely. I felt downright abused by life. At times, if it hadn't been for my faith in God, I don't know where I would be today.

During this silent suffering, I used food to compensate for the deeply rooted pain I was feeling, which obviously led to a struggle with weight gain and low self-esteem. Many of my friends and family today would say, "I can't believe you had a problem with weight!" or "I didn't know that you suffered from low self-esteem! You always seem to be happy, excited, and full of life." Yes, I was all of that on the outside, but, just like the beautiful chocolate Easter bunny, I was hollow inside.

I was constantly putting myself last in order to put others first. I had always been a caregiver. I took care of my mother without help from my siblings, took care of my kids without the help of my husbands, and let's not forget how a wife takes care of her husband. I was the caregiver who helped everyone spiritually, emotionally, mentally, and, at times, financially. Even in my current job, I am a caregiver. But who cares for the caregiver?

I had become the president of the Need-to-Please Club, and my duties left me feeling empty and broken. It was as if someone had hung an Out of Order sign on my neck, pushed me in a corner, and neglected to call the service technician to come fix me. I had nothing left to give. As a caregiver, you are constantly giving of yourself—your time, your energy, your love, your peace of mind. It is easy to become hollow when you are constantly emptying yourself to fill others. If you don't take care to fulfill yourself, you may eventually crumble. I wanted desperately to fill myself once I recognized that hollow feeling, only I made the mistake of filling myself with all the wrong things.

One day I looked in the mirror and saw a strange, overweight woman staring back at me, but what shocked me most was the fear, anger, and grief in her eyes. I was more than fifty pounds overweight, and I had allowed worry, bad habits, and loneliness to grow bigger than the good inside me.

Clearly, my actions were mere reactions to the events taking place in my life. According to the Kübler-Ross model of grief, I had to conquer the phases of denial, anger, bargaining, and depression; only then would I get to a place of acceptance where I could experience balance and a healthy state of being—a place of solace, realization, and healing. It would inevitably prove to be a long, difficult journey for me. I quickly encountered obstacles that made it a struggle to move beyond the question, Are these tragic events actually happening to me? and begin coping with the anger that demanded answers to other questions: Why me? or How is it possible for such a string of tragedies to happen to one person? Of course, there was also the universal complaint, "It just isn't fair!" In order to reach my destination of balance and fulfillment without getting completely lost on this demanding journey, I relied upon my emotional GPS to guide me on the path toward restoration, revelation, understanding, and emotional rehabilitation.

Throughout my life I had always felt that I had a special purpose or calling. Unfortunately, as a result of the events I endured and my defective coping skills, I discovered that I no longer liked the life I was living. My zest for the things that once meant so much to me had faded. A person without dreams will soon perish; I fought to find my dreams again, and, therefore, to live. I decided to write this book one day after encouraging people to look beyond the surface of what they are going through to identify the habits that got them there. I wrote this book for all those who are hollow and looking to be fulfilled. I wrote this book for you.

Hollow is written in two parts:

Part I: The Hollowing takes you through my life before and after forty, my spiritual death as a result of low self-esteem; depression; and my abuse of food, drugs, and alcohol.

Part II: The Filling takes you through my life approaching fifty, my rebirth as a result of strength from God, knowledge, and determination.

Chapter One

HOLLOWED BY LOVE

hollow hol·low [hol-oh] adjective, -er, -est, noun, verb, adverb

–adjective

having a space or cavity inside; not solid; empty…

having a depression or concavity…

sunken, as the cheeks or eyes.

without real or significant worth; meaningless…[1]

THE WORDS ABOVE spoke to my soul as if I had authored that definition myself. How did I get so empty? Where did these feelings of insignificance begin? When did I derail? These were the questions I had to ask myself, the questions I was afraid to answer. But the most important question I needed to ask myself was, Am I ready to own what I might discover about the *real* me?

I wasn't sure of the answer, but I couldn't hide from myself

---

1   *Dictionary.com*, s.v. "hollow," accessed March 27, 2013, http://dictionary.reference.com/browse/hollow?s=t.

any longer. So, I began to pen this book and find out things I had buried so deep that I had trouble unearthing the truth beneath the lies I told myself.

I'll begin my story with the issue that faces too many women today, weight. Growing up I had always been proportionate and never had a weight problem. I vividly remember being called names like One-bone, Long-legs, Slim, and String-bean because I was so thin. Boy, what I would give to be called those names again. At one time in my life the thought of ever growing to a size fourteen was beyond my comprehension. That size belonged to the clothes on the *other* racks. At five feet nine and one-half inches tall I had been blessed with the ability to maintain a size eight to ten and was at liberty to eat anything I wanted. But then again, I hadn't yet experienced the series of traumatic events that would eventually wreck my life like a typhoon, leaving me absolutely empty inside—an emptiness that I tried to fill with food.

I had always been told by my family to watch my weight because it would catch up to me one day. They said it was simply *in our genes*. When I delivered my oldest son, Walter, I weighed 169 pounds. At that time I thought I was extremely overweight and a negative self-image began to form in my mind that would later contribute to my hollowing. Truth be told, today I would write you a check of any amount to be 169 pounds again. Isn't it interesting how life is all about perspective?

The women in my family have a tendency to "square up," as we called it. Squaring up is what happens as we grow older and the curves that once personified our femininity begin to square off from our shoulders through our hips; hence the term we coined for each other: *halfback*. (A halfback is a football player, and you know how large those guys are!) Our father was very statuesque at six feet five inches tall with broad shoulders and a large chest. Our mother was petite in comparison, considering she was a full foot shorter. My sisters and I often poked fun at one another and called each other "halfback." As a child I told my sisters that I would never square up. I was too active, and I hadn't yet developed unhealthy eating habits. Looking back I see how the fun teasing and taunting I endured as a child would later contribute to my low self-esteem as I battled the weight gain that I swore would never come.

After I had Walter I lost two dress sizes, slimming down from a size ten to a size six, and it provided me a false sense of worth. Still, I felt good for the moment, considering I had just rid myself from a physically abusive relationship with Walter's father. We had married young, and the pressure of being a husband and father proved too much for the twenty-one year old. When we were kids he had always been a dear friend, but the stress of adulthood turned him into an abusive drunk. One night when Walter was two I plotted our escape. When my husband came home and passed out after a night of drinking, I stole fifty dollars from his wallet and caught the first train home to Philly. We divorced without much hassle, and life resumed its normal course.

Time passed, life progressed, and I turned twenty-eight. It was then that I met a man who wined me and dined me. He enjoyed showing me off to his friends, and we often got dressed up to go out on the town. He was thirteen years my senior and enjoyed the finer things in life. I looked like a queen, but inside I was already beginning to crumble. I chose this man because he made me feel good about myself. You see, somewhere along the way I became one of those women who looked to a man to make me feel better about myself. I needed them to like me, love me, and be attracted to me. The sad truth is that I desired this attention because *I* didn't like me, *I* didn't love me.

Jackson, we will call him, helped me fill the void in my heart. He told me what I needed to hear, and I looked like he wanted me to look—he was my comfort, and I was his eye-candy. We got married and settled into a new life together.

Shortly thereafter I became pregnant again. As my stomach

grew the numbers on the scale grew. But that's what women do; we gain weight during a pregnancy.

Unfortunately, Jackson noticed that my weight was escalating faster than it should, and he chose to encourage me to eat right by constantly reminding me that his ex-wife was small when they got married, and she ballooned to over three hundred pounds during their marriage.

His words hurt, but I swallowed my pride and tried to convince him that this was perfectly normal. I was his third wife but the first to bear him a child. He didn't hesitate to let me know that his ex-wife's weight gain was the main reason for their divorce. He reminded me almost daily that he didn't marry a fat woman, and he didn't expect to be married to a fat woman after I had delivered our baby. He constantly watched what I ate and monitored my weight gain at each doctor's visit. I remember standing in front of the refrigerator one day looking for something to eat. You know how you just stand with the door open and stare because you can't figure out what you want? Well, I was doing just that when he called out from the family room saying that his ex-wife used to stare in the refrigerator like that, and I should close the door before I ended up like her. His words stung, and each time he made a negative comment I felt him nibble closer to my hollow core.

If it hadn't happened earlier, by this time I had developed a catastrophic relationship with food. Jackson would lash out at me about my weight, and I would seek solace with food to ease the pain of his words. Of course, the foods highest in calories and fat provided the most comfort. I used my pregnancy as an excuse, claiming that I had cravings, and promised to lose the weight after the baby was born.

I had always loved food, but as my weight climbed and my self-esteem descended, my love of food became an obsession with no boundaries. At the time I lived in Maryland, and my sister, Loretta, lived about a half hour north of me. Jackson played golf every Saturday, and on this particular Saturday I devised a scheme to satisfy an uncontrollable urge to devour some soul food. I called my sister and convinced her to ride with me to Washington, DC, so we could eat at the Florida Avenue Grill, a legendary landmark that offers the most authentic soul food your taste buds could ever crave. My intention was to pick up my sister, then drive down to DC to eat, and bring back some take-out to savor for later—all before he got home from his golf game.

The day went just as planned. We ate to our hearts' content and brought home collard greens, potato salad, pig's feet, and, yes, we even got the chitterlings. I was in soul food heaven! I felt good and full and smug thinking about how I had pulled one over on Jackson. Now, he was very old school in the fact that my domain was the kitchen, and he generally stayed out of the way and expected me to fix his meals. However, as fate would have it, the next day he decided to clean out the refrigerator. Perhaps my smug attitude or satisfied smile gave me away, but I realized I was about to be busted for the greens and pig's feet I had hidden in the back of the refrigerator.

I can laugh about it now, but at the time I felt awful; he made me feel awful. He yelled and ranted and raved.

"Did you put pork on my baby's head?" He had been adamant that I didn't eat pork during the pregnancy, and I had the nerve to get chitterlings!

He was furious, and I was guilty. His tantrum lasted for what seemed like forever, and I simply took the verbal abuse. But secretly, I think I was less hurt about his tirade and more upset that he threw out my food.

Things seemed to settle a little between us as I got closer to delivering the baby. I did my best to make him happy by watching my eating habits, although mostly I ignored his comments. Perhaps he even offered his rude comments less often. On October 5, 1990, I gave birth to a second son, Ronald. We discovered that I had been carrying two placentas, which meant that somewhere during the beginning trimester I was having twins and had lost one. Ronald, however, was healthy, and weighed eight pounds three ounces. I weighed a whopping two hundred and ten pounds—the heaviest I had been, but not the heaviest I would be.

Shortly after I delivered Ronald, Jackson lost his job. With his focus on trying to find work he didn't have much time to bully me about my weight. Still, I knew I had to get the weight off soon or the verbal attacks would begin again.

During the winter of 1990 Jackson was still struggling to find work, and we decided to move to Atlanta, where his family lived. I was on maternity leave from the hotel chain where I worked but put in for a transfer. At the start of the new year, while Jackson stayed behind to sell our condo, I packed up the baby and moved to Atlanta.

Until we could find our own place I moved in with my mother-in-law. This woman was not only sweet as pie, she baked the best pies imaginable. As a matter of fact, she could do all sorts of magic in the kitchen. She grew her own vegetables in the back yard and would make my mouth water with her creamed potatoes, greens, creamed corn, and homemade cornbread. Then one day she introduced me to fried peach pies. I had died and gone to food heaven.

I began to eat like this every day. These extravagant meals that reminded me of Sunday dinner or Thanksgiving feasts back home became my everyday treat. When I wasn't eating my mother-in-law's food I was enjoying the restaurants that lined every corner in Atlanta, offering such Southern goodness as macaroni and cheese, greens, fried fish, fried chicken, sweet potatoes, corn bread, and, of course, some good old sweet tea to wash it all down. By the time Jackson finally joined me in Atlanta I had put on another fifteen pounds. I knew I was in trouble.

The baby and I slept in the bedroom; Jackson expressed his displeasure by sleeping in the living room. Our already dwindling intimate life became non-existent. I felt the pressure of our marriage dissolving, and I knew I had to do something—quick. I did what most overweight woman would do: I shifted into *lose weight quick* mode, only I found that there is nothing quick about losing over fifty pounds.

Thanks to my new soul food temptation, it was extremely difficult to lose weight. The curse of the squared-off halfback haunted me. Surely I wasn't destined to be one of *those* women from my family. In my mind, a size eight was just one diet scheme away. I treated my weight gain with back-burner priority, convincing myself that I could get it off. But like most women, while my weight concerned me and I wanted to lose weight, I had no self-discipline, no consistency, and for every time I tried to get on, I fell off the wagon.

By now, I had surpassed the size fourteen on the clothes rack and had moved on to a size eighteen. I was officially and undoubtedly plus-sized. My familiar weight-loss efforts were unsuccessful, and none of the lose weight quick schemes were returning me to my pre-pregnancy size. My yo-yo diets left me feeling like a failure. Jackson complained about my weight and further diminished my self-worth with comments like, "Boy, are you squaring up!" My family added insult to injury as they teased me about reaching the weight I swore I'd never be.

I had to lose the weight. The soup diet. The only-beans diet. The Monday, Wednesday, and Friday-only meals diet. Starving. Fasting. Whatever shed the pounds so I wouldn't have to hear Jackson's belittling comments. Our marital problems and my weight struggles were a heavy burden to bear. To cope with the stress of it all I would alternate between binging, starving, and exercising—nearly passing out in the gym from working out so hard.

I don't think Jackson and I were ever close again after the birth of our son. Even after moving out of his mother's house and into our own home we only had brief moments of happy times (usually centered around my weight loss), but things were never the same. I wasn't the woman he wanted me to be, and his negativity took a toll on me.

By 1996 it was obvious that we would divorce, and we soon did. I purchased a small home and settled in with the boys. I can remember that day the divorce was final like it was yesterday. I walked into the house, drew a bath, and took a long look at myself. I was overweight, single, and raising two sons alone. I recognized that it would be hard for me to recover and start life over as a single woman, especially knowing how society viewed overweight people.

I became more and more accepting of myself as an overweight woman. I was very involved with my sons' lives, worked full-time, and oftentimes we ate late or picked up dinner at the nearest fast food drive-thru. Obviously that wasn't the healthiest choice for me or my boys, and it only led me farther in the opposite direction of where I should have been headed. Not being in a relationship allowed me to drift deeper into my secret obsession with food and my unhealthy habit of binging. Food made me feel good, and no one had the right to take that feeling away from me.

I knew that it wasn't healthy to keep feeding my boys fast food, and I was happy that they stayed active. I went to golf practice with Walter and tennis practice with Ronald. Running with the boys and becoming active in church kept me busy and helped me to begin to lose a little of the weight I had gained, but my life became more un-balanced. I didn't eat healthy because I refused to make quality time to take care of *me*. Everything and everyone came before me.

As the boys got older I started dating again, and that motivated me to start my regimen of dieting, fasting, and starving. It was incredibly difficult to stick to a healthy regimen in my out-of-control, non-disciplined life. I began dating a guy I had known for years. We worked for the same company years prior and had remained friends. He was also a minister, and I felt comfort in loving a man of God. Things were good in the beginning of our relationship, and I continued to lose a few pounds. He encouraged me to eat healthy and work out. However, there was something slightly unhealthy about our relationship. Despite his calling to a higher power, "The Minister," as I'll call him, was superficial, and when it was directed at me it became hurtful. He wanted me to fit an image, and if I didn't match that image he would tell me things like, "Wear your hair long, but don't wear that weave," or "If you're getting your nails done you better have red polish on your toenails."

He also had a problem with commitment. As a minister, he could marry a couple, but he didn't have the conviction to get married himself, although the promise of marriage rolled off his lips easily and often—not only to me but to others. Our on-again, off-again relationship seemed to fit my inconsistent lifestyle of yo-yo diets. Sadly, I was oh-too-happy to settle for less than what I deserved, and so I accepted whatever he offered.

The Minister was the type of guy that would always walk around announcing that he was "the man." Literally. He started out treating me nice. Ladies, you know this type—the man who does whatever it takes to get you, and as soon as he has you, you meet the real person. He was the over-controlling, gorilla-pounding-on-the-chest guy. I used to ask him why he would always announce that he was the man, and he would say, "Because you needed to know." My response would be, "Who are you trying to convince, you or me? I have never walked outside and heard a tree pounding on its trunk saying 'I'm a tree!' It just is a tree and does what a tree is designed to do. So if you *are* a man, just be a man and do what a real man should do."

I always had a snappy comeback when he started with his "I'm the man" tantrums, but the truth was that I didn't feel good about myself during this stage of my life and The Minister was a perfect fit in my imperfect life. The way he treated me and the way I treated myself were one in the same. He only committed to me during the winter months. I joked with him that during the summer he wanted to run and play, and in the winter he needed a warm place to stay. It wasn't as much of a joke as I made it seem. When he was around, The Minister treated me nice enough, and in my warped state of mind I rationalized that his behavior was OK because it meant I wasn't alone. He filled that ever-present void in my life.

However, my weight was still an issue. I was comfortable being pleasantly plump as my weight began to climb again, and the more comfortable I got, the more weight I gained. Because of my weight, there were times when The Minister wasn't *into me*. It became harder and harder to lose weight, and the bigger I got the larger my hollow core became. I remember how sharp the pain was the day he told me he wasn't attracted to me anymore because of my weight.

I started my on-again, off-again diet regimen in a futile effort to win back his affection. This time, I did things differently. I exercised when The Minister complained about my weight. I was careful to do just enough to keep him off my back, and I gave him regular updates about my exercise and eating routines, since he inquired almost daily. I would casually say, "I ate a salad," and change the subject. The truth of the matter was I would eat whatever I wanted and then indulge in my new drug of choice, adrenaline from extreme workouts. Was it as obvious to me then as it is to me now that my life lacked balance and emotional stability? Probably not.

The Minister watched my weight like a hawk and wanted to know what I ate at all times. I accepted his inquisition as a part of the relationship and buried the way it made me feel. I only remember a brief period where my weight wasn't an issue for him, and that was the time I cared for my sick mother. For a change he was simply supportive, since the two of them had gotten along so well. However, my weight was never far from his mind. I knew he loved me, but I had learned that men are very visual, conquerors who feel the women in their lives mirror their accomplishments. I knew he wanted a trophy girlfriend, and I was definitely not that.

My relationship with The Minister went back and forth for years. When we would break up, he would say, "I have decided that I don't want to be in a relationship anymore," or "I woke up today and realized that I don't want a girlfriend anymore." I was always fearful that he would wake up one day and end the relationship again. But my feelings were inconsequential. All that mattered was what he wanted—that's what he believed, and I accommodated him.

I once asked The Minister why he treated me the way he did and why he walked on me like I was a doormat. His answer was amazingly truthful: "I don't treat you bad. You treat yourself bad. I couldn't walk on you if you didn't lie down." My heart was shattered, but what a powerful statement! Every time he left I would lie down so he could wipe his feet on me on his way out, and every time he came back I would lie down again so he could wipe his feet on me again. How many other women are out there doing the same thing—laying down their self-worth just to be in a relationship with a man?

My last break up with The Minister was the day he told me that I couldn't come to his house anymore. Shocked and in disbelief, I asked "Why?" He explained that he was renting the basement of his house out to some lady and her teenage daughter. "What does that have to do with me coming to the house? Are you sleeping with her? Who is she?" He told me he was not sleeping with her, but was hoping their relationship would go in that direction so he wouldn't be able to see me anymore. "Are you kidding me?" I screamed. I may have been a doormat, but I wasn't dumb. I knew he wasn't moving a woman and her daughter in his house with mere hopes that the relationship would become sexual—it already was.

I was furious, outraged, frantic with anger. If the conversation had taken place face-to-face I would have gone to jail and gotten a mug shot for what I would have done to The Minister. I still get angry thinking about it. But most of all I felt stupid and shameful for staying in another unhealthy relationship. I realized, the hard way, that a man of the cloth is not necessarily a man of God.

I believe The Minister actually thought he supported me, but how could someone confuse such negative comments as uplifting or positive? If his *intention* was never to hurt me, his *method* was all wrong. He didn't have a weight problem, so he had no point of reference to measure what I was going through, and I felt that because he was able to eat whatever he wanted without gaining weight he wasn't qualified to make any judgments. Yet I let him pass judgment on me constantly.

So here I was in yet another dead-end relationship. I thought about my broken marriages and how I felt after they ended. Now I was ending another relationship that had managed to pull me down even farther. My self-esteem was at an all-time low. Today I can recognize that a key characteristic of someone who doesn't feel good about himself or herself is making unwise decisions. Through all my inconstancy I demonstrated a consistent lack of good judgment. My decisions about relationships were kin to jumping from the frying pan into the fire.

SUMMARY

Every woman deserves to love and be loved, and that is really all I ever wanted. My problem was that I was looking for these relationships to validate me and fill my hollow space. I now know that I can't look to someone else to fulfill all my needs or validate me; that must come from within. I had to start by remembering and understanding that God most definitely fills me with love, and His is the only validation I need.

I wanted so desperately to be in love that I ended up living in fear of not being loved. The irony is that my fear created the exact situation I was trying to avoid; only instead of being alone and unloved I was in a relationship and still not loved. My emotions dictated my actions and reactions; because of that

I allowed my man to walk over me, disrespect me, talk down to me, and even cheat on me.

Only recently did I discover the root of this self-destructive behavior. I asked myself, *When did I lose respect for myself?* Was I subconsciously playing out a scenario I had seen before? Yes! I had watched my mother stay in an abusive relationship with my father for more than twenty years. I had watched my mother lie down as my father walked out on her many times and watched her lie down when he walked back in our lives. I had watched her deal with infidelity. I had even watched her accept that my father bore two other women three children after my mother had me. I had watched my mother stand by him when he was sick only to have him walk out on her when he got well. I watched her swallow her pride when she walked into his hospital room and saw one of his other women sitting by his bedside.

I knew my father as the head of the household who gave me those beloved Easter baskets. I didn't realize that at the same time I was developing an expectation that his behavior as a husband was normal. I realize now that I had married and dated my father.

On her deathbed I asked my mother why she stayed with my father. Her answer shocked me: "Where was I gonna go? We didn't have it like women have it today. I wasn't educated, and besides, I had seven children I was raising. He took care of us, kept a roof over our heads, food on the table. Where was I gonna go?"

How many women are reading this book asking, "Where am I gonna go"?

Learn to love yourself. Be happy and healthy, and don't allow your current situation to dictate your future. Value your self-worth, because if you don't, no one else will. If a man doesn't want you, nothing you do can make him stay. Whereas, if a man really wants you, nothing you do can make him leave. Never lose yourself while trying to hold on to someone who doesn't care if they lose you. When this happens, you are most likely in a toxic relationship.

Here are just a few tips that have helped me identify when I am in a toxic relationship:

- You can't trust them with your deepest secrets.

- The person smothers you, always wanting an account of where you are and what you are doing.

- They steal your dreams, and they're rarely supportive.

- They are very needy, and you have to work real hard to keep them happy.

- They are merely in your life out of habit. Does he really love you?

- You don't like the person you become when you're around them.

- They drain you of your energy.

- They always put you down to exalt themselves.

- They want you to play by their rules and refuse to compromise.

- They take, take, take, and never give in return.

Chapter Two

HOLLOWED BY DEATH

I N FEBRUARY 2005 I had to rush my eighty-five-year-old mother to the hospital. That day remains one of my most devastating memories. There's a huge knot in my throat as I think about finding her shaking, feverish, swollen, and alone. For her sake I appeared calm, but inside I was terrified.

"Mommy? Mom!"

She was crouched over a bowl of soup, trying to get the spoon to her mouth. She looked up at me and weakly replied, "Hey."

I bent down to kiss her, and she was on fire. Her temperature was so high she was burning up. Thank God I didn't go home that day.

If I had told her I was going to call the ambulance she would have talked me out of it. I snuck to another room, called 9-1-1, and told them my mother was very sick. While waiting for the paramedics to arrive I took her to the bathroom and cleaned her up. My mother was a very proud woman, and I wanted to dress her in a clean nightgown. When the ambulance arrived and they took her vital signs the paramedics said they needed to get her to the hospital right away.

At the hospital they told me her heart was failing. She was transferred to a hospital that specialized in cardiology. Eventually she was diagnosed with congestive heart failure and a leaking valve on the right side of her heart. She spent two weeks in their care. The doctors told me that my mother was too weak for surgery. They were giving up.

I will never forget the words her doctor said that day: "There is nothing else we can do for your mother. Take her home and make her comfortable."

At first I didn't understand what that meant because I always made my mother comfortable. I was in shock. The doctor was telling me to take my mother home, love her, and spend as much time with her as I could because she didn't have much time left to live.

I was still grasping the subtle message: Take her home and make her comfortable because she is about to die. My question to the doctor was, "When?"

"I can't put a date to it. She could be here two, three, five months or so, but her health will continue to decline."

Internally I lost it. Outwardly I had enough sense and composure to prevent my mother from seeing how disturbed I was by the news. I simply followed the doctor's advice, took her home and made her comfortable. I knew I was about to embark on an emotional journey and that my mother would be ripped from my life far too soon.

I was a single mother, and my own mother would need care around the clock. How was I going to care for my mother full-time and pay the bills? Even though I had several siblings who lived in the area, I was the one who became my mother's care-giver in her last days. In the face of such a distressing situation God was good to me; I was blessed with a compassionate boss who allowed me to work from home indefinitely while I cared for my mother.

My mother was a very strong woman. She was known for keeping it real. She shot from the hip and did not beat around the bush. My mother knew what the doctor meant about making her comfortable, and she didn't hesitate to sit me down and give me her thoughts on the matter.

I will never forget the day she said, "Baby girl, time ain't long for me. Soon I will be going home. I need you to help me put my affairs in order. I am going to need you, because no one else in the family will do what I need done."

Pretending not to understand, I asked her what she meant. "How do you know that you are going to die?"

"Baby, I just know. First God prepares a person's mind so they can talk about it like I am doing with you now. And faith comes by hearing. Then He prepares a person's heart so that they will act on it. The thing a person prepares for will come."

"Yes, you are right."

She continued. "I will need your help with my transition from this life to the next. Will you help me?"

Reluctantly, I committed to helping my mother, but I had no idea what I was about to face.

My mother didn't talk about her impending death often, but when she did she laid out clear details. Then she let it go and would live a little. She had me put her affairs in order: policies, insurance papers, last will and testament, power of attorney (POA), and her do not resuscitate (DNR) order. My siblings went through this process from afar, knowing our mother was dying but being able to put it out of their minds when it disturbed them too much. I had no real escape from the truth. I was scared and stressed, but I followed her directions and supported her in anything she asked me to do.

I did have a few friends who helped me take my mind off of my mother's illness. Their names were food and, my newest friend, alcohol. These feel-good friends didn't do much for my emotional state, but the sensation they gave me temporarily filled my hollow. My friends were there for me when others weren't. They comforted me when I was lonely, consoled me when I was sad, and gave me something to look forward to each day.

My life was changing. I was growing stronger and weaker at the same time. My mother, my rock and my advisor, was leaving me. I was strong enough to take care of her, but inside a part of me was dying as well. I functioned in a state of denial. My life was changing, but I fought the change as hard as I could.

That summer my mother's pastor approached me and said God instructed him to honor my mother's eighty-sixth birthday. I thought it was a great idea and would take Mother's mind off the details of her end-of-life affairs. So, we began planning the surprise celebration of her life as "Mother of the Church."

This is what I refer to as *good stress*. Planning a party to honor my mother on her birthday had me on high. The celebration was wonderful. It brought family and friends together, and my mother was very surprised. Her face lit up as she watched the tributes honoring her life. That is a beautiful memory I still cherish; my mother was as radiant as the sun—bright, happy, and full of life.

My mother would tell me, "You can't appreciate the sun until you have had a few cloudy days." It was unfortunate for me that those cloudy days rolled back in soon after the celebration of her life. Shortly thereafter, her spark began to fade.

I noticed physical changes in my mother that I did not understand. When a person nears death they may stop talking or responding and begin sleeping more as their body changes how it uses energy. Although my mother slept a lot, I always assumed she heard me even if she seemed unconscious and did not communicate. I talked to her and rubbed her arm to reassure her of my presence and love for her. At times she seemed withdrawn and focused less energy on the world around her. Most times she only wanted family and her pastors around. These were sad times in my life, times I wish to forget, but then again I couldn't bear to part with the last few memories of my best friend.

The elders of the church say that as people transition they may speak to beings others cannot see or see people and places not visible to those around them. I discovered this truth one day when my mother had a conversation with a tall man she said stood behind me.

"Baby girl, who is that standing behind you? I can't see clearly; I don't have my glasses on. Oh, I know who that is. That's your dad."

My father had been dead for many years, and at this point I was desperately holding on to my own sanity. I did what I felt I had to do. I made an announcement to all the spirits in the house waiting for her to transition.

"Can I get everyone's attention that I can't see? You don't need to come around here trying to get her to come. She's coming, but she'll do so in her own time! Back off, please, because you are freaking me out. Don't come around here. She will be there soon enough."

I joke about it now, but I am not ashamed to say that I was not joking then. By that time my emotions had nearly numbed. I can look back and say that I was *void of reality.* At times I was mad at the world for taking my mother or mad at my siblings for leaving me with such a heavy burden or even mad at myself for reasons I can't recall. But mostly I was just hollow.

As difficult as it was, my mother needed to know she had my permission to go. I've often heard stories of people who hold on even in the face of prolonged discomfort and death just to know their loved ones will be all right. My mother told me that she needed to go so that I could live. During the times I would break down and cry she would comfort me saying, "Don't cry for me; be happy for me. I will be safe in Jesus' arms. Tell everyone who doesn't know Him to get Him off the backburner and make Him first."

In November 2005, after taking her for one of her many doctor's appointments, the doctor confirmed that her time to leave was close, but they continued to give her medications to keep her stable and ease her pain. She was quickly growing tired of the medications the doctors insisted she take. The medications merely prolonged the inevitable. They prescribed blood thinners, heart meds, blood pressure meds, water pills, and pain meds, just to name a few. I jokingly asked her how she was able to keep track of them all. She responded, "It has become second nature."

Soon my mother was taking medications to counter the side effects of the pills that kept her body alive. And then one day she decided not to take the medications anymore. As my mother was released to hospice care she said, "Baby girl, please don't put me away. I want to be here with you when I die. Will you let me die here with you?"

Of course I would. It was important to me that I honor the final wish of such an amazing woman, incredible mother, wife, daughter, aunt, niece, sister-in-law, and friend. I would do anything for my mother. What proved even more beautiful was that as her days dwindled she continued to protect and nurture me. She was still my rock, my advisor, and my best friend.

For some death is very private, and they wait for a brief moment alone to slip away. Others will wait until they are in the company of a select few to let go. I wasn't sure how my mother's crossing over would take place, but one thing I did know was that I did not want to watch her struggle during her last moments. I remember praying, *God, please let her go peacefully in her sleep.*

I experienced an array of emotions, even thoughts of dying myself. This sweet and loving woman wanted to be with me, in my home, when she transitioned. I knew my life would never be the same, but such a drastic change was a lot to endure. I didn't want my life turned upside down. *I didn't want my mother to die.*

As my mother grew more ill, I grew more frantic. I didn't sleep much during this time. I was afraid that I might oversleep and not hear her call if she needed anything. I was tired and weary. Even when I was exhausted, I suffered from anxiety and worry that prevented me from getting actual rest. Food and alcohol offered me some solace but not enough.

Soon, a new friend joined our gang. One day I was helping my mother out of bed for her bath, and as I picked her up I felt an excruciating pain in my back. I didn't have time to go to a doctor, and my mother had numerous pain medications, so she offered me a Percocet. "Perky" became my new best friend.

Perky relaxed me, coaxed me to sleep, and dulled the physical and emotional pain that afflicted me. After my back healed I still kept taking the Percocet. I found myself relying on the Percocet to go to sleep. When one pill was not enough I would take two. When two pills didn't work I'd accompany them with a glass of wine. Food and wine and Perky and denial we were inseparable.

One night after feeding my mother and getting her to bed, I went to my room to turn in. I always dreaded going to bed, because when the hustle and bustle of the day ceased I was left with nothing but the thought that in the next room lay my dying mother. I always went to bed with the thought of, *Will it be tonight?* After so long sleep deprivation is more debilitating than you might imagine. I was nearly delirious with exhaustion. I craved rest. To slow my mind and get some sleep I would take the Percocet and a glass of wine.

This particular night I couldn't ease my worries. I knew the end was getting closer, and my mind was racing. I suffered from both sleep deprivation and anxiety, so I took two pills and had one glass of wine. Then I had another glass of wine. Before I knew it I had practically finished the entire bottle. Finally my body lost its fight for control of my mind, and I passed out. I never heard my mother calling for me. I never heard her ringing the bell that I had gotten her so she could let me know when she needed me. I never heard my dying mother begging for me to come to her side.

The next morning I woke up and went into her room to check on her as usual. When I walked into the room I found her waiting for me, soiled and embarrassed.

"I am so sorry," she said. "I had an accident. I called you and rang the bell, but you didn't answer. I knew you had been tired, so I just thought you finally got the rest you needed."

I was so ashamed. I'm still ashamed. I began to cry and beg for her forgiveness. She was so sweet and understanding, but I could never admit to her that I was passed out. I carry that shame with me to this day.

You see, I totally understood what Michael Jackson was feeling when he took the sleeping medications that eventually resulted in his death. As a result, according to the coroner's report, he died of cardiac arrest and complications from a drug meant to help him sleep. I just wanted to sleep as well. But what I was really searching for was *rest*. I didn't know then, but I understand now, that there is a big difference between sleep and rest. I continued to take things to help me sleep, but what I was really chasing after was rest and peace. I needed rest from all of the stress of planning my mother's end-of-life affairs. I needed rest from the sadness of planning my mother's funeral. I needed rest from the hardship of being a caregiver.

As we approached Thanksgiving I found myself cooking a lot and hoping that my mother would be able to eat, hoping that the holiday would be as normal as possible. There are many great cooks in my family, starting with my mother, and it was heartbreaking to see that she was unable to contribute because she was so weak. The holiday was already depressing.

My mother was able to enjoy her Thanksgiving dinner, and the family was thankful that she did. Food was important to her, and she loved to cook, so we gauged how sick my mother was by how she ate. On this day she ate, but very little. Family and friends visited to see mother as we approached what would be her final days.

I cherished this time with my mother, and we had wonderful conversations. As she opened up to me it became easier for me to help her plan her going home celebration. She expressed to me what she wanted to wear, saying, "I want to be dressed in all white and would like to wear a real nice suit." She picked the color of the flowers she wanted on the top of her coffin. We even picked out the color and style of the coffin she wanted. I vividly recall that it was called *White Cloud,* and it was pure white with pink trimming. She and I worked side by side planning the program, everything from the scriptures to be read to song selections. She loved Proverbs 31 and wanted me to read it because she had patterned her life after it:

Who can find a virtuous woman? for her price is far above rubies. The heart of her husband doth safely trust in her, so that he shall have no need of spoil. She will do him good and not evil all the days of her life. She seeketh wool, and flax, and worketh willingly with her hands. She is like the merchants' ships; she bringeth her food from afar. She riseth also while it is yet night, and giveth meat to her household, and a portion to her maidens. She considereth a field, and buyeth it: with the fruit of her hands she planteth a vineyard. She girdeth her loins with strength, and strengtheneth her arms. She perceiveth that her merchandise is good: her candle goeth not out by night. She layeth her hands to the spindle, and her hands hold the distaff. She stretcheth out her hand to the poor; yea, she reacheth forth her hands to the needy. She is not afraid of the snow for her household: for all her household are clothed with scarlet. She maketh herself coverings of tapestry; her clothing is silk and purple. Her husband is known in the gates, when he sitteth among the elders of the land. She maketh fine linen, and selleth it; and delivereth girdles unto the merchant. Strength and honour are her clothing; and she shall rejoice in time to come. She openeth her mouth with wisdom; and in her tongue is the law of kindness. She looketh well to the ways of her household, and eateth not the bread of idleness. Her children arise up, and call her blessed; her husband also,

and he praiseth her. Many daughters have done virtu-
ously, but thou excellest them all. Favour is deceitful, and
beauty is vain: but a woman that feareth the LORD, she
shall be praised. Give her of the fruit of her hands; and let
her own works praise her in the gates.

—PROVERBS 31:10–31

She was a virtuous woman. The last days of her life were both
challenging and life-changing for me. It was at this time that I
began to find out who *I* was and the very nature of who I would
become as a woman. There was a scripture in the Bible, John
12:24, that helped me cope with what I was facing: "Verily, verily,
I say unto you, Except a corn of wheat fall into the ground and
die, it abideth alone: but if it die, it bringeth forth much fruit."

My mother and I both knew that this scripture was our destiny. She was dying, and the process was going to bring forth
much fruit in me. She would always encourage me during
this time saying, "Baby girl, what doesn't kill you makes you
stronger. You have what it takes to make it in this world. You
can do anything you set your mind to. Take care of yourself;
eat right, lose weight, and remember to reward yourself, which
is what I failed to do in life." These words echoed loudly in my
hollow soul.

Around this time my mother took off her wedding band, the
one she had worn for as long as I could remember, and the
mother's ring she designed herself. She put them both on my
fingers. I knew the significance of her handing me her most
precious sentimental jewelry, but denial nudged me, and I
asked her to hold on to them, assuring her that I would take
them when I felt the time was right. I didn't want the time to
ever be "right" for something so wrong.

I knew the time was nearing when I would have to say good-
bye to my mother. I dreaded it and prolonged it. I knew that
letting my mother go would be a tremendous expression of my
faith and the greatest gift I could offer her. Saying good-bye

to my mother and allowing her to transition peacefully meant that I had to trust God. In church we always talked about *trusting God*, but what did the words really mean? To me, at that moment, it meant: Do you really trust God to take care of the person that He trusted to take care of you? God had entrusted her to me as a gift, and it was my turn to present this wonderful gift back to Him. Call me selfish—I didn't want to gift her back to Him.

Loved ones called or stopped by to say their good-byes. I still hesitated. She was my best friend, and I loved her. I still couldn't bear the thought of parting with her. Eventually, I gathered the strength and faith to say the words that haunted me. With a good cry and a loving kiss I released my mother from my hands to God's arms. She was His to take at any moment. While I was happy that she would soon go to meet the Lord, I was left with a hollow core so profound that it would take years to fill.

Mother woke up very early on a Tuesday morning as she did every day, but this day was different. She started off by requesting to see her pastors.

"Baby girl, I want to see Pastors Riley and sweet Kay. Call them and tell them I want to see them."

I called the pastors and asked them to come to the house right away. When they arrived and my mother saw them, she lit up like Christmas morning. "There they are! I just want to tell you how much I love you and to say thank you for introducing me to Jesus and teaching me His Word. You put the Word deep in my heart, and I love you for it."

My family and another minister from her church were also there. Mother began telling Kay how much she loved her. Kay sang her a song, and everyone joined in unison. Mother began to tell us each how much she loved us and told us all to keep God first in our lives. Everyone sang her favorite gospel songs with her. She prayed with us and *for* us. I was amazed at her strength—as her life was ending she put her prayers and energy into blessing the lives of others.

My mother then asked us to turn the lights down in the room, saying it was too bright. However, there were no lights on and only minimal light coming in from a single window. She repeated her request a few times, then her expression changed and she lifted her arms toward the ceiling, looking as though she were watching something there. She prayed aloud and then suddenly stopped. With both arms lifted as if being summoned, she said, "Oh Jesus, You are so beautiful! Oh, my God, you are so beautiful, my Jesus. Your face is so beautiful."

My mother's face was exalted. I had never seen her as excited as she was at that moment. Her lifelong dream, the thing she hoped for most, had come to pass. Jesus, her Lord and Savior—the one she sang to, prayed to, and told her troubles to—had just revealed Himself to her. I don't dare doubt that she saw Him in all His glory.

After glimpsing something so magnificent, my mother must not have wanted to stay in this earthly realm much longer. As the day progressed, more family members called to say good-bye, but mother spent most of the day asleep.

The next day she slept without waking up. We talked and sang to her, but she never opened her eyes or responded. I once heard a pastor teach that we are spirit beings living in a body and possessing a soul. I believe that the day before, with her arms outstretched, my mother's spirit went into Jesus' embrace. I believe that her spirit was no longer with us; she had already gone to be with the Lord and therefore she couldn't speak. Her physical body was simply going through its natural process of shutting down.

I looked at my mother that day, and I knew it was time to remove her rings as I had promised. I kissed her softly on the hand and removed her wedding ring, which I placed on my left hand and her mother's ring, which I placed on my right hand.

"I love you, Mommy," I told her. I was empty inside.

On Thursday, December 1, 2005, my beautiful mother

drew her last breath and transitioned to the place she sang about—heaven.

She often said, "All I want is a corner in paradise." Once she developed a relationship with God and became a born-again Christian, she would then say, "God, I don't want just a corner in paradise, I want a mansion!"

I am confident that she is in paradise, in her mansion enjoying a life free from diabetes, heart disease, high-blood pressure, and the side effects of all the medications prescribed to control those debilitating disorders.

I was a mess, but what kept me sane was the fact that my mother spent the last month preparing me for one of the most stressful times I would ever face. I am grateful that she spent her last days building me, encouraging me, and pouring wisdom into me. It was during that month that I began to find my true self. Still, it would take a few years to fully walk and live in my new discovery.

Christmas that year was difficult. It was my first Christmas without my mother. I was deeply depressed. Although I returned to work, my spirit was somber. I merely functioned at the most basic level—eat, sleep, work. Not only had my mother been an active part of my life, she had been my *entire* life for the past month; now I came home and she wasn't there. Often, I would sit in her room or I'd go to her closet and smell her clothes. I missed her so much. I still miss her.

I wanted a new beginning for the new year. I started 2006 with a fresh outlook. If I could just pull it together I would be OK. I managed to pull myself out of my depression long enough to focus on regaining the life I lost when I lost my mother. Unfortunately, I started the new year with old habits. Once again I was in a cycle of starving and fasting and exercising. I did manage to lose about twenty pounds, and it did wonders for my spirit. Of course, I was inconsistent and undisciplined as usual, so it was simply another quick fix with temporary affects.

The possibility of my finishing a project or reaching a long-term goal was a joke.

I am great at starting something, but when life throws me a curve ball I look for every possible reason to cop out and give up. If only I had understood that *consistency* was the key to a breakthrough I wouldn't have struggled nearly as hard.

When my mother left me I became responsible for yet another member of the family. My fifty-one-year-old sister, Furnice, suffered from paranoid schizophrenia. Furnice had mental challenges for as long as I remembered. She was the third of the seven children born to my parents. Prior to her diagnosis she had been in and out of hospitals, jails, and drug rehab centers. She had been considered a problem child until her diagnosis when she was in her twenties.

Furnice lived in a nursing home in Pennsylvania. While my mother had been sick I spoke with Furnice's caseworkers and told them that my mother had been given little time to live. The caseworkers told me that Furnice was already on a suicide watch because of severe depression, and they suggested that it was best if we held off telling her about Mom for fear that she might hurt herself. I took their advice and waited, but I think Furnice knew, somehow, that our mother was sick.

The May after mother's passing I received a call from Furnice wanting to speak to our mother and to wish her a happy Mother's Day.

I stammered, "Mother can't come to the phone, but she loves you very much." It was the only thing I knew to say.

"OK," my sister said. "Tell her I love her too and will see her soon."

I cried all day after speaking with her. A few weeks later I received a call from my sister's caseworker informing me that she was doing well and seemed to have bounced back from her bout of depression. They felt she was strong, and it was a good time for me to tell her about our mother's passing.

I was relieved; keeping our mother's death a secret from my mentally ill sister had been a heavy burden to bear. At the same time, being charged with telling my sister about our mother was an equally heavy burden, and I was a nervous wreck. I pleaded with my family to go with me, but they all declined. I went to the airport, boarded the plane to Pennsylvania armed with my mother's strength, and prepared for the visit.

When I arrived it was so good to see my sister. We both shared a good cry followed by lots of laughs as we looked at photos of our nieces and nephews, many of whom she had not seen since they were young.

But finally, I had to say what I dreaded. I began telling Furnice how much our mother and I loved her and that there comes a time when we all grow old. I explained to her that our mother turned eighty-six on her last birthday and was having a lot of problems with her heart. Then I said, "Furnice, Mother went to heaven in December. She is there right now guiding me through this conversation with you and wants me to let you know how much she loves and misses you."

Furnice was remarkable. Of course, she and I shared a good hard cry, but to my amazement she quickly stepped into her role as an older sister and comforted me. I was beside myself with grief. Grief over our mother's passing, grief over the secret I kept from my sister, grief because Furnice didn't have the chance to say good-bye to Mother. But more than all that, I was livid because I had to do all this without the help of any of my siblings.

Furnice was saddened by the news but showed an unpredictable emotional strength and wisdom. She gave me a tour of the nursing home, introducing me to the nurses and telling them all that our mother had gone to heaven. I didn't fully understand it then, but there was a warm calm in her spirit that she hadn't exhibited in ages. It was like she knew something that I didn't, and now it was her turn to keep a secret.

SUMMARY

Being a caregiver is a tremendous responsibility that offers little recognition. In today's society many people find themselves with the exhausting task of taking care of their children *and* their parents. Many caregivers experience depression and emotional stress on top of the physical ailments like sore muscles and exhaustion. If you're a caregiver with little or no relief, it's imperative that you find time for yourself, and if you've already reached a state of depression (which often lasts long after the passing of the loved one) then please, for your emotional sake, seek help!

The responsibilities of a caregiver are physically, mentally, emotionally, and even financially taxing. I knew my mother loved me and appreciated the energy I put into her care, but many days I couldn't help but be worried, frustrated, sad, and overwhelmed.

If you're a caregiver or you know someone who is caring for a loved one, I can't stress enough the importance of building a support system of positive people. As a caregiver, you have to find time to take a break, or you will suffer the physical and psychological ramifications. One of the main reasons I wrote this book is because I didn't have the resources available to help me with the task of providing full-time care, and I want to help the next person.

Even when hospice sent someone over to help with baths and other minor care, it was too little too late. By then I was hollowed and sleep deprived and addicted to the company of food, drugs, and alcohol. Instead of seeking professional help, I told all my troubles to a bottle of wine and my good friend Perky. I hope to be able to provide you with some sound advice to prevent you from experiencing my lowest moments.

You know when you're on a plane they tell you that in case of an emergency put your own oxygen mask on first before helping children or others? Being a caregiver is the same concept. It's not selfish to find time for yourself; it's logic. If you're irritable, tired, or sick, then you can't provide the best quality care. So take some time to find a moment to care for yourself, and you'll be able to better care for your loved one.

CARE FOR THE CAREGIVER

- Check with your county for resources available to the elderly or sick.

- Don't be too proud to accept help or ask for help.

- Join a support group (even if it's an online group or chat room).

- Take time for yourself—exercise, read a book, soak in the tub, etc.

- Plan ahead.

One of the most incredible things my mother did was plan for her future. When she accepted in her heart that her time was near, she began to put all of her affairs in order. She had her DNR, insurance policies, and will complete. Although it bothered me while she was still alive, afterward I was grateful that she had gone so far as to plan the details of her service. When she finally passed the only thing I had to do was execute her wishes. Having all those affairs in order are crucial to preventing even more heartache during a time of grief.

Chapter Three

HOLLOWED BY THE CHURCH

church [church]

noun

a building for public Christian worship

a public worship of God or a religious service in such a building...

the whole body of Christian believers; Christendom

any division of this body professing the same creed and acknowledging the same ecclesiastical authority; a Christian denomination...

that part of the whole Christian body, or of a particular denomination, belonging to the same city, country, nation, etc.[2]

---

2   *Dictionary.com*, s.v. "church," accessed March 27, 2013, http://dictionary.reference.com/browse/church?s=t.

That He might present it to Himself a glorious church,
not having spot, or wrinkle, or any such thing; but that it
should be holy and without blemish.

—EPHESIANS 5:27

I WAS DRAWN TO this scripture for the opening of this chapter,
but I had to ask myself, What does it mean when the Bible
mentions a "church without spot or wrinkle"? Is it referring
to the actual building being without blemish, or is it referring
to the body of people? My interpretation of this scripture is that
it is about the body of people. Sadly, Christians often use this
scripture to refer to a building. I can't believe that Jesus, whom
the above scripture references as the one who will present Himself, is looking to present Himself to a building, no matter how
glorious it may seem. Yet many Christians believe that the
church is merely the building with the steeple and cross on top.

If Jesus were to come back today searching for a *glorious
church* to present Himself to, I'm afraid He'd be lost and utterly
appalled. Oh, don't get me wrong, He would find many splendid
buildings with beautifully stained windows, ornate decora-
tions, and steeples with crosses on them. But He'd find very few
believers without spot or wrinkle.

Before you take offense to my words, understand that my
love for God dates back as far as I can remember. I grew up
in the church, although later in life I realized that the church
I grew up in was one that spent more time praising the bishop
than honoring the Lord. The church called non-members
"outsiders." Few people joined the church or married into the
church; you were born into the church. Growing up, we weren't
allowed outside influences like movies, and our lives revolved
around the bishop, whom the congregation all referred to as

Daddy. Yes, it had cultish qualities. That was where my mother had believed she could only have a corner in paradise. When we left that church and she learned the true power of God, Mother understood that God had a bigger and better plan for her life. Through it all, we loved God.

After all the hollowing I had been through in my life, I decided the perfect refuge and opportunity for healing would be to work for God, in His house. I ended up working for two mega churches and consulting for several evangelistic associations. My expertise was marketing and television programming. For years I owned a consulting company that helped churches and evangelistic associations increase their presence in their communities and assisted them with producing Christian television programming. I traveled nationally and internationally, hosting seminars and developing church leadership. I have seen much and experienced more. By the time I dissolved my company, I had been hollowed by the misrepresentation and misappropriation of the "church."

I never questioned God, but whenever I've questioned the motives of the men and women behind the pulpit I've been answered with hostility. I believe God to be a loving God who wants to help us understand Him. I believe my purpose is to help people have a better relationship with God. But I have learned, through firsthand experiences, that pastors are merely human and like us all they are susceptible to greed, vanity, lust, and deceit. My wish for you is that you learn to trust God for yourself and recognize when those leading the congregation have gone astray themselves. *Follow me as I follow Christ*—recognize when you follow a pastor who isn't following Christ.

As much as we'd all like to hold our pastors on a pedestal, the fact remains that there are corrupt, dishonest practices and a general lack of integrity at the pastoral level in some churches today. Is it an epidemic, or has it always been this way? I can't say when or how the corruption began, but beware of the pastor who uses their congregation for their own financial gain and praise the pastor who sets aside their own needs for the needs of their congregation.

I have talked with numerous people who have experienced the hurt of their church's corruption firsthand. I have been on the inside of church organizations that have asked me to help them build memberships and partnerships with people purely for the possible profit. I have been asked by church pastors to assist with organizing crusades, conferences, and meetings, all with the intent of generating financial support for their personal gain and satisfaction. I have sat in meetings where the topics weren't about the sick and shut-in or the members in need but instead centered on how much money came in through the PO Box that day and how to generate even more money. Rather than determining what scholarship to set up or what ministry to create, the questions were, What gimmick or sad story can we offer to get more people to empty their wallets? Can we sell oil, prayer cloths, jewelry, or even prophecies from God Himself to drive up revenue?

Don't get me wrong, I understand that a church has to pay the mortgage and that the power company or phone company doesn't do charity work. But I'm not speaking of money to cover operating costs; I'm talking about lavish lifestyles that directly contradict the mission of the church. I've seen the unnecessary trips taken on private jets with friends and family using tithes and offerings while the congregation worried about how to feed their children. I have watched pastors cajole people into digging into their pockets yet again because "God said that there's one thousand more dollars to be collected today." I watched the pastor stuff his pockets while the congregation emptied theirs despite their unemployment, foreclosures, children who couldn't afford college, and mounting debts. I've seen pastors take advantage of the congregation's financial needs and—in some cases—their financial greed by promising fruitful returns for the money that was donated.

During my initial consultation when working with an

organization I would ask for a copy of their vision, mission statement, or statement of belief. To my surprise, many didn't have them, or those who did requested things of me that didn't line up with the ideals they claimed to follow. At this time in my life my consulting business was my sole source of income; still, I turned down several accounts because they went against my moral and ethical beliefs. I couldn't in good conscience be part of corruption and deceit. I knew those churches weren't operating for the Lord's will; they were operating for their own.

Pastors would often want to show me around their church during this initial consultation. I would tell them that I didn't need to see the building—I just wanted to attend service. That's the "church" I would assess. I wanted to worship with their congregation, and from there I could tell them what worked and what didn't. I likened it to a hospital. What good is an elaborate building if the doctors and staff don't heal the people who come for help?

In December 2006 I took a job with a church that had the appearance of great integrity. They said all the right things and projected all the right images. I trusted the organization and its pastor; even though accepting the position required me to move and make some major changes in my life, I was happy to do so.

As soon as I was on the inside of the organization I discovered that they weren't any less greedy than the other organizations I had shunned. They were just more skillful in implementing their deceitful tactics. They would have several offerings during the service "in the name of God" to get more money out of the congregation over and above the normal tithes and offerings. They requested more and they required more of their congregation than any other church I had worked for before them. People were sold hopes and dreams from the pulpit with a straight face, while in the back office they were spending the money as fast as it came in—and not on operating costs but personal luxuries.

This church profited greatly from the presence of celebrities and athletes that sat in the pews. They were a nationally televised megachurch, and everything they did was for the cameras; anyone who was remotely famous sat front and center, and the cameras would pan that way often so the world could see. There was a special room behind the pulpit where they took new members. The room was covered from ceiling to floor and wall to wall with pictures of the pastor alongside famous people. This was their way of manipulating people into believing that they must be special if they joined the same church these celebrities visited or joined.

When I was approached to work for this church I was informed they needed my expertise to help facilitate major changes within the executive office. Once I arrived and started asking questions about things I discovered, I was labeled as a person to watch out for because I asked too many questions. I took my job seriously. I was professional and ethical. Little did I know that doing my job well would land me in a world of misery.

The church had a dedicated group of people working for them, but it always felt odd to me, like they were groupies who craved the pastor's attention rather than the Lord's. I was often approached by someone who would ask me, "What's your story?" What I discovered was that most of the people who worked for the church had a story that involved being rescued by the pastor. They were all misfits before belonging to the church. In their previous lives they had been drug addicts, pimps, prostitutes, and convicts, and in their new life they were showered with luxuries for turning their lives over to the Lord. What they failed to realize is that they had merely turned their lives over to the pastor, and in return they offered their service without question. They believed that the pastor—not God—had saved them. Too often, when someone has blessed us at some point in our life, even if we deserved it or earned it, we then feel obligated to overlook their wrongdoings in an effort to continue to show our gratitude. This church had learned how to capitalize on that unyielding gratitude.

This church was well known. Christians and non-Christians alike know the church well. You can catch the pastor on TV any given Sunday. They appeared to be the pinnacle of the twenty-first century church, making strides and developing new ways to use technology to spread God's Word. But the one thing they lacked was God Himself. I began to discover inconsistencies with policies and procedures. Where there were no policies or procedures I was told "that's just how things are done here." If they broke any ethical or legal rules, I was expected to look the other way. I wasn't very good at looking the other way; I was too disturbed by what I saw. I wasn't looking for any of these discrepancies. They just showed up each and every day, and they were too unethical to ignore and still sleep at night.

My conscience wouldn't let me stand by, so I met with the senior pastor to discuss some of my findings and review new policies and procedures I had developed to correct the issues. I had been encouraged to write a report and submit my findings, and I naively thought this meant they were ready to address the issues. In actuality, it earned me the label of not being a team player and, worse yet, sparked an investigation about my character. When I met with the pastor I realized that because I couldn't be bribed or bought, their only recourse was to threaten me.

"I even know where you stopped for coffee this morning. I'm watching you," the pastor warned me.

It was true. I was told that they knew where I lived and how I spent my time. They knew when I came and when I went. One day I went to visit a friend and noticed that I was being followed by an SUV. My friend lived on a dead-end street, so when I pulled in to her driveway we stood outside to watch the car come down the street to see who was inside. It was one of the church leaders. I was angry, but, more so, I was fearful. Years later I received confirmation from a security company that they also had tapped the office phones, and it was suspected that the company-issued cell phones were also monitored. I wanted to bide my time slowly and have the next job in place before I made any rash moves. But I knew I had to get out and get out soon!

The job became so stressful that I would sit and cry in my bathtub with the water running so my son wouldn't hear me. My oldest was on his own, but my youngest was doing great in his new high school and I didn't want to concern him. I was tired and angry and fearful and stressed. I worked nearly seven days a week. My job required me to attend every service, which left little time to spend with family.

To make matters worse, I had developed the worst eating and sleeping habits of my life. With this newly added stress and still lacking discipline, I ate my way through each series of stressful events that took place. Still, the worst was yet to come.

I discovered some shocking news about the senior pastor regarding an illicit affair that would later be written up in nearly every major newspaper and aired on a multitude of news channels. Armed with the information I had discovered, I chose the high road, and rather than profit from anyone's misdoings I brought the information to the pastor so it could be rectified before it was discovered by others.

I knew that this information would be detrimental to my career. They would either try to draw me closer or push me out the door. Either way I was in for a rough battle. The day came when I was called in to the office and told that I didn't fit in and, effective immediately, my services were no longer needed. I was escorted to my desk to retrieve my purse and asked to leave the church property. In April 2007, a mere four months after starting my job with this church, I found myself unemployed.

I was heartbroken and downright pissed off! I had interrupted my life (although it was somewhat dysfunctional already) to relocate and work for a church—God's church, so I thought—only to be faced with even more dysfunction.

After bad breakups, losing my mother, and moving to a new city, I was now without a job. I had hit a new low. I had heard about people dealing with depression, seen the commercials on TV, but depression was a whispered word in the black community. It couldn't be happening to me. And yet, it did. I went from being busy seven days a week to sitting at home with nothing to do. I got up each day with my son, made breakfast before he went to school, and when he left I went back to bed. I stayed in bed all day except when I ventured in the kitchen to cook one of my outrageous meals, like pumpkin pancakes, shrimp and grits (my absolute favorite), or fried *any*thing. I would bake cookies, eat pizza, drink sodas, and go back to bed. I didn't drink just a glass of wine; I drank the bottle. I would get up each day just in time for my son to get home from school, cook dinner, and try to act "normal." I was hurt, depressed, hopeless, and completely hollow. The most frightening part of it all was that I had no idea how to snap out of it.

I cried a lot. I was in an unfamiliar city, and I missed my best friend, my mother. I once heard someone say that you have to fight depression each day and recognize that it's a daily process. That's true, but what happens when you have no energy to fight? Most days I only had enough energy to pull the covers back and invite depression to get in bed with me. Oh, there were days when I fought like there was no tomorrow, but most days I just existed.

When I would recount this story, many people asked me, How does a Christian allow herself to get empty? How can you be a Christian and be depressed? Why didn't you go to your church and ask for prayer, aid, or assistance? My answer was quite simple: *because the church was responsible for part of the hollowing!* I know that I am not the only person that has been hurt by the church. I've met several people who have experienced some form of betrayal at the hands of the trusted members or pastors of their church. How many times have you reached out to the church for prayer, called the church to speak to a counselor, or asked for assistance, only never to have your phone call returned? For me, it is too many to count. Or maybe you've heard this line: "I'm sorry, you are not a member at this church. We only counsel, help, aid, or assist members that pay tithes and offering."

I felt like I was losing my mind, but I was sane enough to know I needed to talk to someone. One day, feeling desperate, I reached out to a pastor that I had done some work for previously. I had not seen him or done any work for him in about two years, but I had found him honest and a true man of God, so I picked up the phone to call.

The church administrator answered the phone and told me that the pastor was out of town but assured me that she would give the pastor my message. Within two days I received a return call from him. Tearfully I told him what had happened to me and what I was going through. Without hesitation he said, "My wife and I will go into prayer about this situation."

I was so glad he wanted to consult his wife and that they would pray together with me and for me. It didn't stop after that phone call. They continued to pray and counsel me through that difficult time in my life. Other times they just let me vent and talk through my emotions. They didn't care that I wasn't a member of their church, didn't ask me when was the last time I paid tithes and offerings. They didn't even ask me when was the last time I prayed before calling them. Their only care was that I was hurt, lonely, broken, and depressed but still a child of God, a sister that needed help. They wanted to ensure that I got the help that I needed. I thank God for Pastor Bank and Sharon Akinmola—they held my hands through some tough times and some very lonely nights.

I hope I've been clear that my testimony here is not an anti-church rant but rather a request to open your eyes and make sure your pastor is walking in the same light he/she is directing you to walk. Too many people have been scarred by the organization and its people that offer healings. Church—the body of people *and* the building—should be a place of filling, not hollowing. How do you stay filled when the shouting and dancing are over? Make sure that you are energized by the congregation and pastors of your church, and rethink your church home if you are left feeling drained.

Too many church organizations have become mere social networks, the who's-who of church life and Christian social clubs. We have forgotten the true reason we should come together is to pray for one another, lift each other up, and encourage our brother or sister. You should be filled with the love of God, not emptied by the greed of man (or woman). Make sure that your church is truly a church of God.

Do not forget Jesus' mandate in the New Testament:

> And he answering said, Thou shalt love the Lord thy God with all thy heart and with all thy soul and with all thy strength and with all thy mind; and thy neighbor as thyself.
>
> —LUKE 10:27

And certainly don't forget that in order to "love thy neighbor" we must first learn to "love thyself."

SUMMARY

How come some folks that shout on Sunday morning are depressed on Sunday night? What happens when church doesn't work?

We have become more concerned about how we worship than who we worship. The very place that was designed to heal us can hurt us when we don't hold the church board accountable. There were times in my life when the place where I should have felt safe, the church, rejected me, and therefore I rejected me as well. The Bible tells us in several Scriptures to put our trust in God, not in man, and warns us to beware of those who will come in the name of the Lord to deceive us.

- Mark 13:6 "For many shall come in my name, saying, I am *Christ;* and shall deceive many" (emphasis added).

- Luke 21:8 "And he said, Take heed that ye be not deceived: for many shall come in my name, saying, I am *Christ;* and the time draweth near: go ye not therefore after them" (emphasis added).

- Matthew 24:11 "And many false prophets shall rise, and shall deceive many."

- Jeremiah 14:14 "Then the LORD said unto me, The prophets prophesy lies in my name: I sent them not, neither have I commanded them, neither spake unto them: they prophesy unto you a false vision and divination, and a thing of nought, and the deceit of their heart."

- Matthew 7:15 "Beware of false prophets, which come to you in sheep's clothing, but inwardly they are ravening wolves."

- Matthew 24:24 "For there shall arise false Christs, and false prophets, and shall shew great signs and wonders; insomuch that, if it were possible, they shall deceive the very elect."

- 1 John 4:1 "Beloved, believe not every spirit, but try the spirits whether they are of God: because many false prophets are gone out into the world."

There are numerous scriptures to support my advice that it is important for us to view our lives as God sees us, not as man would see us. In hindsight, I should have focused my energy on how God saw me instead of being hurt by rejection from a corrupt church.

I commend those pastors who are out there changing lives and truly helping their members. For those who are not, consider your ways. I plead with you to consult your moral compass and the moral compass of those whom you follow.

Laypeople and ministers, if anyone with authority over you, whether at church, home, work, or school, asks you to do something that goes against the grain of your moral and ethical standards—don't do it. Remember, anything you compromise your values to keep, you will eventually lose.

I learned that lesson when I put my trust in people, knowing I should have put my trust in God. Many people have been hurt by church, and they blame God for what man has done. Remembering how God sees me changed my perspective. God didn't hurt me; people hurt me. People will always have the ability to hurt you. God will only love you. In God's eyes, there is no judgment, hurt, or pain; there is only acceptance.

> The LORD is my rock, and my fortress, and my deliverer;
> my God, my strength, in whom I will trust; my buckler,
> and the horn of my salvation, and my high tower.
> —PSALM 18:2

God saw light in me when all I could see was darkness. He loves me more than anyone could ever love me. He loves me as I am!

Chapter Four

HOLLOWED BY GRIEF

I<small>N</small> M<small>ARCH</small> 2007 I received a call from my sister, the next to the oldest girl in the family. She shared with me that her son had been diagnosed with cancer of the liver, and things did not look good. Our family was disheartened by the news, but we hoped and prayed for his recovery. My nephew was thirty-six years old, lived in New York, and was what I referred to as a wandering soul. He did what he wanted to do and lived a fast and hard life. "It's the way I want to live," he would say.

He had been in and out of the hospital with cancer for months before being given the news by doctors that there was nothing else they could do for him. The news was heart-breaking, a tremendous blow to my sister and our entire family. My nephew was my sister's only child, and now she was faced with watching him leave before her.

A few months later he was released into hospice, and the family braced for the worst. Not knowing how much time he had, my sister went to New York to be with him. One morning I woke up (one of the days when I could actually get out of bed) and decided that I needed to be with her as his condition worsened. He was getting close to the end, and I didn't want her to be alone. It's one thing having to deal with the death of our mother, but having to prepare for your only child's death—I couldn't imagine what she was experiencing. I often heard my mother pray, "Lord, please don't ever let me look down on any of my children." Her prayers had been answered, and she didn't have to bury any of her children. Being the mother of two wonderful sons, this was something that I too prayed I would never have to experience.

My sister updated me on my nephew's condition, "Not good at all. He's not responding, but with the medications he is resting."

I knew in my heart that he would transition from our lives soon, so I jumped on the next plane for New York. When I arrived he was mildly coherent, but he knew I was there, which gave us false hope for a miraculous recovery. Our hopes were quickly dashed the following day when his health declined rapidly. On June 22, 2007, my thirty-six-year old, handsome nephew drew his last breath. His mother and I stood in tears at his bedside along with a nurse and a priest, who prayed for my nephew as he transitioned.

As I stood there grieving I began to understand things my mother had said to me just before she died.

"You will need to be strong; the family will look to your strength in the future."

"When you feel like you can't walk anymore, God will be right there with you to carry you."

"God will never leave you alone."

"You are stronger than you think. If you are never tested, you will not fully understand what you've learned."

"Take care of your sisters and help them as much as you can."

I understood these things, and yet I felt no stronger. After the passing of my nephew I was in the worst condition of my life. I felt all alone, but oftentimes I heard the sweet voice of my mother saying, "You are stronger than you think. You can't break, because the family needs your strength." I didn't feel strong; I didn't want to be strong. I was confused and hurting and hollow. I could not handle anything else; not right now.

Shortly after my nephew's passing, in August of that same year, I received a call from my sister Furnice. The doctors wanted to perform surgery on her knee to alleviate her severe arthritis. I spoke with her caseworkers and doctors and agreed it would be a great opportunity for Furnice to proceed with the surgery so she could be free of pain. We educated Furnice about the surgery, and everything was all set.

Then I received a frantic call from Furnice. "I don't want to have this surgery. I'm afraid I won't wake up."

I tried to convince her that it was normal to feel this way. I assured her that she was just experiencing a little anxiety and that most people have the same fears just before surgery. I comforted her by explaining that the mind doesn't always comprehend things, and sometimes it plays tricks on us by creating unnecessary fears. I didn't know if any of what I said was true, but it sure sounded good.

I didn't manage to convince her, and she was adamant that she didn't want to go through with surgery. She was not obligated to do anything she wasn't comfortable with, and I had no intentions of forcing her. In fact, I told her that if her knee began to hurt too much I would buy her a scooter so she could be more mobile. She didn't want the scooter either but conceded that she would reconsider the surgery if the pain worsened.

A few weeks later Furnice called to wish me happy birthday and to share a bit of good news; after talking with her caseworker and doctor again she decided to proceed with the knee surgery. I told her I would be there to support through the surgery and visit with her in the hospital until she returned to the nursing home.

I flew up to Pennsylvania a few days later and got to the

hospital just as Furnice was coming out of surgery and being taken to her room. She was doing great and feeling fine. I kissed her and smiled, knowing that she'd be relieved of all that pain.

The next morning she was recovering well. The doctor had removed the IV, she was sitting up, and she was eating solid foods. We played games, talked, read books, and laughed. The day was special for us both, and I looked forward to her release in just a few short days. As I was leaving her that night to head back to my hotel room she asked that I go to Walmart and get her some "smell-good stuff," such as perfumes and lotions, as well as her favorite candy, Jolly Ranchers.

"Of course! I'll bring them tomorrow," I said, and I kissed her on the forehead as I left.

I returned to the hospital the following morning with an armful of goodies for my sister. When I arrived I noticed that her personal belongings were sitting outside of her room. I asked a nurse if Furnice had been moved to another room, and she told me that during the night my sister had taken a turn for the worse and was moved to the Intensive Care Unit (ICU). I was shocked. *Turn for the worse? ICU? But she had been doing so well!* I pleaded with them to let me know what happened and demanded immediate answers. The staff took me into a conference room and asked me to sit and wait for Furnice's doctor. They wanted to prepare me before going into her room.

My heart was pounding, my stomach was knotting, and my mind was racing. *How much more could I take? How much more would I be asked to take? What could have happened between my leaving the night before and returning the very next morning? What was I going to see?* The doctors and nurses were vague, and I hoped her condition wasn't as critical as they were leading me to believe. Soon enough they let me go to ICU to see for myself.

I walked into the room prepared for the worst, but what I saw was much worse than what I expected. My beautiful sister was lying on her back with her hands strapped to the sides of the bed. There was one tube inserted in her mouth and another in her nose. The lump in my throat got bigger until I was almost choking on it, and then I noticed the horrible sound—a sound I still can't get out of my head—of that ominous machine breathing for her.

I kissed her gently on the forehead, and she opened her eyes. When she saw me she began to cry. I began to cry. Her eyes were wide with fear and confusion. I felt her eyes begging for answers to questions she couldn't speak: *Where am I? What's happening to me?* I spoke to her first with my own eyes, trying to soften them behind the tears to help her be unafraid. Then I spoke softly, comforting her, telling her that she was OK and assuring her that I would take care of her. She nodded her head indicating she understood.

That day I stayed at her bedside and watched them battle her blood pressure. I counted fourteen different bags of "stuff" they were pumping into her. Her blood pressure continued to drop throughout the day. I have never seen nurses work as hard as they did to maintain her blood pressure.

I called my family to tell them the news. We were all so fragile, but I was nearing a breaking point. I couldn't do this alone. I had taken care of my mother a year prior, had to go tell Furnice that our mother passed, lost my job, stood by my sister's side as her son took his last breath, and now I was alone while Furnice fought for her life.

When my mother said the family would need my strength, it all made sense now. But how could I give them something I didn't feel I had? I needed someone from my family to be with me. I called my sister Vanessa in Philadelphia, who lived about two hours away.

"I can't do this by myself. I need to have someone else here with me. Please, *please* drive down here."

Vanessa and my niece KrisCynthia arrived, and we all stayed by Furnice's bedside until she was stabilized. Around 2:00 a.m. the nurse encouraged us to go back to our hotel to get some rest and promised to call us if anything changed. We all left, but as soon as we got to the hotel I realized I couldn't sleep. The three of us decided to take shifts sitting with Furnice at the hospital. I anxiously took the first shift.

When I arrived at the hospital around 6:00 a.m. I sensed something wasn't right. Furnice was in worse condition than when we left a few hours ago. The nurses said she began to decline rapidly earlier that morning. I asked Furnice to squeeze my hand if she heard me and knew I was there. To my surprise, she did. But an overwhelming feeling came over me that she was going to leave.

It was at that moment that the words from her Mother's Day phone call to our mother came back to me, "Tell Mommy I love her and will see her soon." I remember the secret she seemed to carry in her heart when I had visited her to tell her about our mother's death. Had Furnice known all along that her time with us would get cut short? And then I felt something that I can't quite explain. I sensed that my sister was trying to connect with me to say good-bye. *Oh my God, could this really be happing? Is my sister about to die?* Anger and grief flooded me, and tears spilled over my cheeks. *Why, why, why is this happing? Please God, why?*

I remembered watching my mother's body begin to wear down as her spirit prepared to leave, and a sick feeling of déjà vu came to me as I watched my sister on the bed before me. I cherished those last moments with Furnice.

The doctors came to do their rounds, and they announced that she had about a 10 percent chance of survival. They were simply being kind; I knew she was already gone. My sister had stopped responding. The doctors felt that the best thing for her would be to remove her from life support and allow her to go peacefully. They offered little hope that she may ever be anything more than a vegetable if she survived. For a brief moment, I was comforted knowing that she told me good-bye. Then suddenly I became furious. It wasn't fair! Their words disgusted me, and I hated the expectant glances in their eyes as they looked at me—the person who held the power of attorney—to give them permission to end Furnice's life.

I was sick, confused, terrified of making the wrong decision. *Did I talk her into having the surgery when she said she was scared and afraid she wouldn't wake up? Was this all my fault? What if she recovered? What would she want me to do? Would she want me to fight for her? If it were me I would want someone fighting for me! How could I live with myself knowing that I had to make this decision? How can I kill my sister? How do you do that?* The questions echoed in my head, and the guilt they brought with them made me want to throw up.

I didn't want the responsibility of making this decision. *Why me? Why me, again? As the youngest child in my family, why did such heavy burdens lie on my shoulders?*

I had called Vanessa and KrisCynthia to come back to the hospital. When they arrived I relayed the grim news and told them what the doctors advised. They broke down, and I heard my mother once again: "You are stronger than you think." I felt no stronger; still, I trusted my mother. I called the rest of my family to give them the same news. We wanted the doctors to fight to save her, but the more I thought about it the more I realized that I couldn't bear to watch my sister endure much more.

The family discussed Furnice's situation, and with great remorse we all agreed with the doctors. I let the doctors know our decision and that it had one condition: If she began to breathe on her own, then the doctors must fight to save her life.

The time came to remove the tubes. They allowed us to be with her, and we stood close waiting on bated breath. We watched solemnly as her heart slowed to a stop. Within two minutes my sister flatlined, and the beeping became a shrill, steady sound, announcing that she was gone—another sound I will always remember. She slipped away sweetly. We stayed with her as they cleaned her up, and each of us cut a lock of her beautiful, curly hair.

In our hearts we had done the right thing, but it provided little comfort for our weary souls. With the death of my nephew only two months prior and Mother's the year before, the family felt that none of us had the heart to endure another funeral process, and we decided to have her cremated instead.

The next day I went alone to the funeral home to identify her body when it arrived from the hospital. My body and mind were numb, but my stomach was weak and my heart was enraged. I sat across the table from the funeral director as he began to explain what they would do and what I had to do and how much money they would need from me that day before they would even touch her. I pulled out my credit card and handed it over the table. I didn't care anymore. I couldn't care.

The tears had been replaced by seething anger. *Why am I doing this by myself?* I was still recovering from the heartache of caring for my mother alone, and I was still unemployed. My brother and sisters offered no emotional or financial support. Why was I alone yet again when death's servant sat across the table from me nickeling-and-diming me while offering false sympathies? I was livid. At that moment Mother's voice came to me yet again: "Everyone is not built like you. God knew what He was doing when He selected you for this task. This is what you were born for; remember, when you can't walk anymore God will carry you if you just lean on Him." Her words calmed me and strengthened me, and I found the will to sign document after document confirming my sister's death.

Back at the nursing home I was left alone, yet again, to pack up my sister's belongings. I had never imagined returning to the nursing home without Furnice. By the time I went to her room they had already cleaned it out and moved all of her things to the basement. I found the boxes with her name on it and began to go through years and years of her personal belongings. For each box I emptied my soul became a little emptier as well.

Her caseworker found me shuffling through boxes. He had come to express his sympathies and tell me that Furnice had entered one of her crocheted quilts into a county arts and craft show. Furnice had her eyes on the plaque she wanted to win but never got a chance to learn that she had won first place. The finality that she never knew she won and would never get to know hit me hard.

I was catching a flight home out of Maryland and the drive there from Pennsylvania was two hours through beautiful, rolling countrysides. Typically the drive would be peaceful and put my soul at ease. On that day I could only think about driving my car off the side of the road into a ditch in hopes that no one would find me. I didn't, but the thought was with me for the entire ride.

I was a zombie by the time I boarded the plane. *What just happened to our family? A week ago I boarded a plane to go see my sister. Now I'm boarding a plane knowing I'll never see her again. Did I just remove my sister from life support? How on earth am I supposed to pick up the pieces of my own life at this point? How can I possibly move forward after a week like this?* The questions saddened me, but I realized that I must be stronger than I thought. I had been tried and tested, and the fact that I was still standing affirmed that my mother had been right—even if I felt weak and fragile at the moment.

I had cried so much that by the time I arrived home my sobs had ceased, and all I had left in me were a few tears that leaked from the corners of my eyes when I thought about sweet Furnice. My body, my soul, my heart, and even my tear ducts were exhausted.

A few days after returning home I received a notice in the mail that my sister's cremated remains were at the post office. *My sister was in a box? My sister was waiting at the post office?* I picked up the box, but I couldn't open it. I didn't open it for a long time. It sat in the dining room, where I rarely entered. I wanted to make it to the next day, and I feared that if I opened

that box I'd lose my will to live. The box sat unopened while my
heart was wide open and felt all the pain of lost loves.

By the time the holidays rolled around that year I had enough
to look forward to that I was able to ignore the pain of the past.
Christmas was fast approaching, and I was overjoyed that I had
reached that time of year when no one watches what they eat. I
had countless excuses to indulge in cookies, cakes, pies, eggnog,
and holiday feasts. I was just one of nine million overeaters
who promised themselves, "I will start my new diet at the first
of the year." To add to my joy, my eldest son was getting married in January, and I adored my daughter-in-law-to-be. Life
was good again.

The only thing plaguing me was the idea of finding a gown
for Walter's wedding. I procrastinated because of my weight,
and I dreaded shopping. The wedding colors were mocha and
tan—colors that made me look old and fat, and to top it off I
felt old and fat. I went to dozens of stores, and I only found the
mother-of-the-bride horrors, boring dresses with the matching
jacket that make anyone look huge. I was disgusted when I
looked into the mirror. I looked like a big square chocolate
candy bar! Finally, I broke down and called my son and asked
him if I had to wear the colors of the wedding or if I could vary
it up a little. Thankfully, he granted me permission to get anything I wanted. My shopping spirit was renewed, and I found
an attractive purple dress that fit me well. I even passed up a
few holiday cookies just to make sure I didn't show up at the
wedding looking like Barney.

The wedding was absolutely beautiful. I was so happy for my
son and his new wife. I felt uplifted and light. When you feel
good, you look good—or at least I thought I looked good until I
saw the pictures. If only I had lost a *few* more pounds. Needless
to say, the New Year began with more yo-yo dieting.

It was late spring when I received a call from my brother Matthew letting me know that his wife of twenty-eight years was gravely ill and in the hospital. The two of them had been renting my home in Atlanta, and I had just spoken with my sister-in-law Alma earlier that week about a few household details. Before I even had a chance to react to my brother's call I received word from Loretta that Alma had passed away.

Alma had grown up with us in Philly, and she was like a sister to me. She and my brother had been married for twenty-eight years, and Matthew had never lived alone. He went straight from living at home to being married. I couldn't imagine how he would be coping with the loss of his wife.

I drove back to Atlanta and helped my brother pull things together for Alma's funeral. They'd had such an endearing relationship and spent so much time together; my heart was breaking for my poor brother. I had always admired the way he referred to her as "his girl," and I wanted desperately to help ease the pain of losing her. He was struggling with the funeral arrangements, and I heard my mother's voice, "Your family will need you." As always I found the strength that I still swore didn't exist, and I did everything I could to ease the burden my brother was carrying.

There was something else I was carrying too: a lot of extra weight. The pastor's mother-in-law stopped by to pay her respects, and when she laid eyes on me she exclaimed, "Oh my, Lynette! Why did you put on all that weight? Girl, you got big!"

Sometimes people don't realize what they say, even after they say it. I was embarrassed, but I had learned to joke about my weight, and so I quipped, "Well, I got down to Florida and discovered the Cuban sandwich. I was hooked!"

It was a fail-safe, quick-wit response. Unfortunately I didn't feel so witty when I could barely button my skirt for the funeral and had to purchase a new shirt because I couldn't close my suit jacket.

My youngest son was preparing to graduate high school.

Although I knew that he would not be attending a school in Florida it hadn't yet dawned on me that he would be leaving me so soon. By the time I returned home my son would be heading back to Atlanta in just one short month. For so long I had taken solace in knowing that no matter how rough things got in my life I could always come home to my son Ronald. The thought of him leaving me was a terrible reminder of how hollow I was; my empty-nest syndrome could be renamed "hollow-nest syndrome."

I needed a distraction and decided to plan a pool party at our home in Florida for Ronald's graduation. In addition to getting my mind off of his leaving I had just devised another opportunity to overeat and drink; after all, it was a party. We invited friends from Florida and family from Atlanta. Because we had so many out-of-town guests, the party lasted for days. My mind stayed occupied, and my stomach stayed full.

But all parties come to an end eventually, and when this one ended I had to face the reality that my son was moving away just two days after his graduation to report for his summer job in Atlanta. At forty-six years old I would be living alone for the first time.

I found temporary work with an organ-procurement company. After dealing with so much death in my life I had found the absolute worst place to work while I was trying to begin the healing process. We would have weekly staff meetings to discuss potential donors—discussions about who was on life support and who was about to die. I cried in those meetings nearly every week. Each discussion forced me to relive the pain and guilt of having to remove my own sister from life support.

The nurses and doctors I had to deal with as part of my job were all accustomed to autopsies and death, but I hadn't yet learned to be so clinical about the end of life. Each conversation was torture. Typically I did not have to see any of the organs we procured for patients, but one day we were asked to discard a kidney (which happens from time to time for various reasons). The nurse coordinator called upon several of us to demonstrate proper procedures for discarding organs. When I saw the kidney I couldn't help but think about the poor person who just lost their life and their still-grieving family. I felt sick; it was time to leave this job.

In my search for a new job I decided to move back to Atlanta. I had been living in Florida with no family and for a job I no longer had. It made perfect sense to return to Atlanta. I began talking to recruiters at my old job, Turner Broadcasting, and landed a wonderful job working for NBATV.

Life was good again. I was moving back to a place I could call home. I would be near family—especially my two boys— and I would be working for a company I truly enjoyed. *I am back where I belong.* It was August 2008.

I had just moved to Atlanta, I was about to start my new job, I had just celebrated my forty-seventh birthday, and I was embarking on a cruise to the Bahamas with my family. I was on top of the world. Then my world came crashing down when I saw a picture of myself on the cruise. I had been happy for a change, and I didn't realize that my weight had ballooned. I asked my son, Walter, who had taken the awful picture of me, "How did I get so big?"

He answered earnestly, "Mom, I thought you knew. Don't you look in the mirror every day?"

I was shocked at the audacity of his brutal honesty, and yet it made sense. Yes, I looked in the mirror every day. How had I *not* noticed the weight? Perhaps it was because I didn't have a full-length mirror, or possibly my distorted body image was distorted toward a skinnier self. Or, more likely, I was too scared to own the truth.

It didn't yet dawn on me that I had failed to effectively allow myself to go through the natural grieving process, and while I was feeling good for the moment I had been on an emotional rollercoaster for nearly two years. Time after time I tried unsuccessfully to fill my hollow core with food, drugs, and alcohol.

Nothing had been filling, and my hollow grew larger as I continued to gain weight.

My weight problem became more than a cosmetic concern when I got ill on the cruise and the ship doctor said that my blood pressure was high. I was sick the entire trip. We visited Paradise Island, and I was exhausted. I became the killjoy of the trip. I was too tired, too hot, too sick, and too embarrassed to walk around in a swimsuit.

I spent a good portion of the cruise in my cabin lying down trying to stay cool. I beat myself up wondering how I allowed my weight to get out of control. In the same moment I was wondering how I gained so much weight, I'd make my way to the midnight buffet to devour ice cream and cakes. Then, in case I hadn't done enough damage, I would take food back to my cabin and continue to binge in private. At some point between wiping my mouth and reaching for another éclair I realized I had an addiction to food.

Food gave me the same euphoric feeling as drugs and alcohol. I had often referred to it as "feel-good food." When it smells good, looks good, and tastes good—I felt good. Binge eaters truly experience a high, a rush of endorphins that are characteristic of that high feeling other addicts crave. Many addicts begin abusing their drug of choice during a period in their life when the euphoria helps distract them from physical or emotional pain that they are enduring. I was trying to fill my hollow. I was addicted to food.

SUMMARY

People grieve in different ways. I chose to eat and drink my way through my grief. I realize now that when I felt my family had abandoned me during my mother's and sister's deaths they simply processed their grief by becoming distant and removing themselves from the source of the pain. I was especially hurt that my brother, my mother's only son, refused to visit our mother during her illness until the last minute. I saw how it hurt my mother, and I was outraged that he could be so distant and callous. What I didn't understand was that my brother was grieving in his own way. Sometimes we tend to want everyone to see or do things the way we would, and it's hard to accept anything different.

I had a hard time accepting my family's different grieving processes. I thought they should have been right by my side going through everything I was going through. I thought that would have made everything all right. But in hindsight I realize that my mother already understood how each of us might grieve, and that was why she had been so unyielding when she demanded that I handle her end-of-life affairs. She selected me because she saw strength in me that I hadn't even seen yet. She had told me once as I was complaining that I wasn't getting any help from my siblings that God knew what He was doing when He gave me to her.

My mother and father had married when my mother was twenty-one years old. They were anxious to begin their family, but they tried to have children for ten years with no success. Although you would think that after a decade of bearing no fruit one would consent that they were barren—not my mother. One night she prayed to God, saying that she didn't care how many kids He gave her but to please bless her with her own children. God answers prayers. Over the next decade my mother and father proved to be very fruitful. In ten years my mother got pregnant nine times. The first four children were girls, and the fifth child was a boy. They didn't stop there. Their sixth child was a girl, Loretta; however, she only lived to be three months and died of crib death; today they call it SIDS. Their seventh pregnancy would end in a miscarriage. The eighth child was another healthy girl, and I was the ninth and last pregnancy. My mother told me that after I was born I "shut the door." God had given her seven beautiful children, and she was done having babies.

She reminded me of this story every time I had asked her why she kept having babies after having the first five. She used to say, "If I stopped having babies you wouldn't be here, and I had to have you." She said that I had been chosen "before the foundation of time" to handle her last day's events and to be there to handle issues with our family. I told her that I didn't want the responsibility because it came at a major price. I expressed this to her on several occasions, and she would always respond, "You are stronger then you think. You can handle this."

I understand now that my family hadn't abandoned me; they were simply grieving. We all went through our own private hell as we faced the loss of our mother, nephew/son, and our sister. My pain wasn't any worse than theirs, but at the time I was resentful I had to be the "strong" one, and I couldn't understand why they weren't there with me. Death takes a toll on all those involved, and while I hadn't realized then how hard my siblings were taking our mother's death, I can see now that we all suffered.

If you are suffering from grief or know of someone who may have just lost a loved one, give them some time to process the five stages of grief according to the Kübler-Ross model, commonly known as the five stages of grief.

- Denial

- Anger

- Bargaining

- Depression

- Acceptance

Denial is the difficulty accepting what has happened. *Anger*, which I knew all too well, is the phase where the survivor questions the fairness of the loss. *Bargaining* is when they ask for more time with their loved one. I bargained with my mom, "You have to be around for my birthday," or to see my first grandson.

Depression is self-explanatory and can last indefinitely if the survivor doesn't grieve properly. I was very depressed for years and withdrew from everyone. Finally, *acceptance* is when you come to terms with mortality. For me, acceptance only came after spending time with God.

If you are experiencing the loss of a loved one, seek support from friends or family or even a therapist. Talk with friends, seek help from someone at your church, or even join a support group. Most importantly, give yourself time and permission to grieve. Prolonged or delayed grief can be very unhealthy—physically, mentally, emotionally, and even financially.

PART II

THE FILLING

Chapter Five

FILLED WITH GOD

P AST FAILURES AND present predicaments had me disoriented. Like a rat in a maze I was searching frantically for some end to this struggle, but I kept hitting dead ends. I was running out of hope. I was tired and lost. Many days I asked myself how I got where I was. Where was God? Why did He let these things happen to me? What did I do to deserve this? I was severely depressed and had long ago begun to think that my own death would be the easiest solution to the problems I could no longer face, let alone solve.

I tried to describe what I was feeling to Loretta one day. "It feels like my brain is Jell-O in my hands. The Jell-O is melting, and each day I cup one hand under the other in a pathetic attempt to keep the Jell-O from slipping through my fingers."

I just couldn't seem to snap out of it and get it together. I had succumbed to despair and had accepted that my fate was to be overweight, addicted to food, and on my way to becoming an addict of drugs and alcohol.

One day at the height of my despair I was in my car listening to the gospel station when Dorinda Clark-Cole started singing "So Many Times." As I listened to the words of the song, I realized how true her words rang in my life. Sung in first person, the song is a reminder to focus on the times when God has come through for us in our past. These testimonies stand as evidence that when we needed Him most, he rescued us from confusion and from circumstances that beset us. As the singer sang of God's redemption in her time of need, I began to think of times when He interceded on my behalf.

So many times God had stepped in right when I needed Him, even when I was too absorbed in my own sorrow to realize it. You see, I had often felt that God had left me, but this song began to fill my heart and refocus my mind. I was reminded of God and His unconditional love for me.

I began to cry uncontrollably, a wailing cry with tears that streamed so heavily I had to pull over on the side of the road. It was the type of cry that slumps you over and makes your face hurt. Yes, the ugly cry. I had cried many times over the past few years, but this time was different. This cry was cleansing. I needed to let it go, and it didn't matter that I was in my car on the side of the road; something was happening to me. I needed to let it happen.

I had been so weak for so long, but with each tear that fell I felt stronger. With each verse Dorinda Clark-Cole sang, I felt stronger. She just kept singing over and over that whenever she was going through all the things in her life she would call on God, and He would come to her rescue. I felt so empowered by what she was saying. It dawned on me that each time I had wanted to stop living, stop hurting, and end my own life, He came to my rescue. It was God's love and strength that got me through each event in my life. I heard my mother again saying, "When you feel like you can't walk anymore, God will carry you."

As the tears slowed I knew that I had to hear that song again. It had been a long time since I owned any music by the famous Clark sisters or their mother, Mattie Moss-Clark. I drove to the nearest Best Buy and purchased Dorinda's CD *The Rose of Gospel*. I knew there was a message for me from God on this CD, and I listened to it the moment I got back in the car. I sat in the parking lot listening to song after song, and I began to pray and thank God for rescuing me from myself. I thanked God for blessing me with Dorinda's gift of uplifting music. I have no idea what Dorinda was going through when she wrote the lyrics to her songs, but I was blessed that she wasn't ashamed to share it with me. I even found divine order in the way the songs were arranged on the CD, and I saw a path laid out for me.

- "Great Is the Lord"
- "So Many Times"
- "Nobody but God"
- "Everything He Promised"
- "Work to Do"
- "For the Rest of My Life"
- "Say Yes"
- "I've Got a Reason"
- "Worked Out for My Good"
- "I'm Out and Over"
- "The Word Becomes Flesh"

This CD began my recovery. It was affirmation that God loves me. Each day I would wake up to this CD and sing each song aloud to remind myself of God's greatness. I felt His love in Dorinda's music, and it warmed my soul.

God had never abandoned me; it was I who had forgotten Him. Sometimes we get so overwhelmed with our issues that we forget some of His greatest attributes. When I think about my mother I think of her with many attributes. I knew her as a daughter, a sister, a wife. I knew her as a mother, an aunt, a sister-in-law. I knew her as a grandmother. These qualities all represent the same person but different roles. There were times that she was in her grandmother mode, and there were times when she was a sister to her only brother. There were times when she was just a friend to someone. There were times when she was a nurse and provider for her children, and there were times when she was a lover to my father.

God also plays many roles in our lives, and it is up to us to acknowledge those roles. I had to understand and know that God is everything to me. He is my advocate and almighty God. He is my answer and atonement. He is beautiful and my blessed hope. He is my bright morning star. He is a burden bearer. He is cleansing to me, and He is a comforter. He is compassionate and complete. He is my confidence, and He is a counselor. He is a deliverer and a door to life. He is excellent and faithful. He is my fullness, and He is gentle and kind. He is good and great. He is the head of the church and my helper in all things. He is hope when I am hopeless and joy when I am sad.

He keeps me when I feel unkempt, and He is a lamp when I am dark. He is bread when I am hungry and living water when I am thirsty. He is the lover of my soul because He is love. He is a mediator when I need it, and He is merciful. He is near and never far. He never fails me. He is patient with me, and He gives me perfect peace. He is my physician, as He is the potter that created me. He is my protector and my provider. He is the quieter of my storm and the refiner of my life. He is my refuge and my rescuer.

He restores my soul. He is the rock of my salvation and my satisfaction. He is security, shade, and shelter. He is a song to me and a tower of strength. He is understanding, my victory, and my vindicator. But most of all, He is the Word of Life to me. He is my God! Remember to thank Him for waking you up each day, and everything else in life can be fixed!

If we only ask He can deliver us from turmoil. I had been so focused on my misery that I had failed to see how He delivered me. I began reading scriptures, remembering lessons my mother had taught me, and realizing how blessed I had been despite my suffering. Most importantly He began to fill that hollow that had been growing inside of me. I felt myself becoming whole again.

Chapter Six

FILLED WITH (GOOD) FOOD

I ONCE HEARD THAT 50 percent of winning a battle from addiction is to first admit it. So I did. Hello, my name is Lynette Jackson, and I'm a food addict.

I decided that anything worth having is worth working for—and working hard. I wanted a better life, and I was finally ready to change by making the right decisions and managing those decisions.

It was time to take inventory of my life. When I finally looked at myself in a full-length mirror I couldn't deny my weight any longer. I stood naked in the mirror, and I saw everything I had ignored for years. I was ashamed at how I had let myself go. I looked old, and I felt older. It was time to weigh myself, but I didn't have a scale. I did, however, have a Wii Fit game that had sat collecting dust since I received it for my birthday. I took the game out of its wrapper and popped it in the console. I first had to create a Mii, an animated version of myself to use for Wii games. I created a cute and skinny Mii chick with sunglasses, eye makeup, and a cute hairdo. She personified who I wanted to be, and I named her Lady J. I stepped onto the game's scale, and a voice on the game said, "Measuring, measuring..." I waited anxiously. "Your weight is 245 pounds. Your BMI [body mass index] is 38 percent. You are obese."

Obese? My first reaction was to throw the Wii out the window. I had never been called obese. Then again, I had never been so heavy. I had most definitely squared up. How had I not realized my fear had come true? *I was square.*

My brother Matthew was living with me at the time, and he asked me what the Wii said I weighed. I was embarrassed, but I told him. He exclaimed, "Wow, look! It even changed your cute little skinny Mii into a fat person!" I cringed.

I knew that if I failed to make changes immediately I would be like so many other members of my family relying on blood pressure, heart, and diabetes medications just to survive. Amazingly, that silly video game was a catalyst for major changes in my life. The Wii was yet another mirror, and I could no longer hide from the obese truth in front of me.

During my first week at the new job with NBA TV I befriended Jeremy Parker, a coworker whom I confided in about how bad I felt after my birthday vacation and my Wii discovery. I said to him, "If I could only lose twenty pounds, I know I would feel better." He told me he could help me lose the weight by sharing his eating and lifestyle plan. He has let me share this plan with you:

Time to Eat	What to Eat
8:00 A.M.	2 egg whites 1 cup plain oatmeal
10:00 A.M.	protein shake
12:00 P.M.	¼ sweet potato plain 1 cup of baked chicken (seasoned with Mrs. Dash only) broccoli
2:00 P.M.	protein shake

Time to Eat	What to Eat
4:00 P.M.	1 cup of brown rice 1 cup of baked chicken (seasoned with Mrs. Dash only) broccoli
6:00 P.M.	¼ sweet potato plain tilapia (seasoned with Mrs. Dash only) broccoli
Anytime	water small handful of almonds between meals when hungry

Like any food addict, I looked at the list and saw restrictions. Oatmeal? The only oatmeal I enjoy is an oatmeal cookie! What, no salt? Salt is all natural. Doesn't that make it an herb? A shake? Now we're talking! I think I'll have my favorite Oreo milkshake from Chick-fil-A or Dairy Queen. I was informed that "shake" meant a protein shake, not ice cream. This sounds like a diet to me.

I thanked Jeremy for the meal plan but told him that all the foods I love were being taken away. I wanted a plan that could incorporate hot wings, pizza, cookies, popcorn, fried chicken, and pasta (oh Lord...no pasta). "Brown rice?" I said. "Who eats brown rice?"

"People with low blood pressure and no diabetes issues eat brown rice," Jeremy retorted.

"Funny, but I don't see bread, and I don't see butter."

"You don't need any butter."

"What do you mean I don't need any butter? Everyone needs butter." God made cows and butter came from the milk of cows; hence, butter must be good.

"You don't need butter."

"OK, can I have Diet Coke?"

"No" he said firmly.

"OK, can I at least fry my tilapia?"

"No."

"So I have to bake tilapia?"

"Yes, or steam it."

I quickly declared that I didn't see how I would be able to conform to this meal plan. I didn't see coffee on the list, and I must have my coffee. "You don't want to see me if I don't get my morning coffee."

"You can drink herbal tea."

This wasn't looking good. At least I liked broccoli and sweet potatoes.

"Remember," he said, "you can't have any sugar or butter. You have to eat your sweet potato plain."

"Who eats a sweet potato without anything on it?"

"Well, you don't have to eat anything from the plan. You can just stay the way you are. But if you are serious about losing weight and changing your life, you will make the effort to do so."

"Wow. Well, if you put it that way..."

On that same day another coworker, Michelle, shared some words of wisdom her mother had told her: "You will never change your life until you change something you do daily. The secret of your success is found in your daily routine, and your life becomes better *only* when you become better. There is no success without sacrifice."

After Jeremy and Michelle told me off I found myself at home that evening looking in the mirror, and I got so mad at my image that I told myself off too.

"You have a chance to live again, and you are complaining about the plan?"

I'm a firm believer that beauty begins on the inside. I knew I had to do some internal cleansing. I needed to spend time reflecting on love, life, and good relationships. Making the connection between my emotions and my eating was one of the most critical realizations that I would make in my recovery from food addiction. I had to evaluate where I was and where I wanted to go. As I began to admit my shortcomings and be honest about what I needed, the most amazing thing happened: I discovered something in the mirror that I hadn't seen before—*me*.

The woman in the mirror was not pretty at all. I saw a garden that had once been beautiful and was now filled with bitter fruit, weeds, crabgrass, and parasites. I hadn't cared for my garden. I allowed my garden to wither and become overgrown with harmful elements. I had experienced so many storms in my life, and rather than deal with the debris I let it pile and fester. I didn't deal with it until it was too late. Instead of pruning my garden of the negatives I had sown bitter seeds of excuses, blame, and childish complaints.

I blamed my ex-husbands, ex-boyfriend, children, job, church, family, and anyone or anything else that was part of my life. I had blamed everyone until no one was around for me to blame anymore. I was lonely from blaming everyone for my self-inflicted issues. Of course I had many tragic events that shaped my life, but it was the way I chose to deal with them (or rather, not deal with them) that had become my biggest problem.

It was time for a reckoning. I had to be honest with myself. I broke myself down and told myself off. Then I said aloud that I loved myself. It was important for me to face my issues and break myself down, but it was equally important to build myself back up. I had to acknowledge that I needed help. I conceded that food, drugs, and alcohol had not been the good friends I had allowed myself to believe they were. I needed God; only He could help, and I looked to Him to help me find the discipline to succeed.

Armed with a healthy meal plan, a new outlook, and God on my team, I was ready to take on the challenge of making permanent, positive changes in my life. I was ready for a complete physical, emotional, and spiritual transformation. I took time to:

- meditate on life using scriptures from the Bible,
- surround myself with people who had life goals,
- keep positive music playing,
- educate myself on nutrition,
- go to bed at a reasonable time,
- create a vision board,
- reward myself weekly with something good to eat,
- rid myself of haters and naysayers,
- change my physical environment, and
- evaluate my relationships.

These were the changes that got me started. However, I continued to add other activities to my life that kept me focused on my goals. Metaphorically, I put on blinders and stayed focused on my race. Once you start a life makeover, the distractions will come. You have to move forward and not be diverted. My distractions came often, but I stayed true. To whom much is given much is required!

On September 1, 2008, I began the filling of my physical body.

It takes twenty-one days to form a habit. I needed to make it twenty-one days on the new meal plan before it could become a way of life. I figured that if I could survive the first week without wanting to kill someone I was sure to make it the other two weeks.

I took my meal plan to the store and purchased the right foods. When I thought about the fact that I couldn't add anything to my sweet potatoes I said to myself, "These ain't my mamma's sweet potatoes." There is nothing in the world like coming in the house to the smell of good food cooking, and there is something real special about the smell of sweet potatoes. I think it is the sugar, cinnamon, nutmeg, butter, and allspice—boy, I am getting hungry! My mamma's sweet potato pies were known throughout the community; she used to sell them at church and in the neighborhood. You know a pie is good when people are willing to pay for it. My momma used to say, "You can't forget to cook with love." My sister-in-law and I used to try to re-create her recipes once she was too ill to bake, but it was hard to re-create a pie made with "a little bit of this" and "a little bit of that."

My son Walter considered himself a sweet potato pie expert. He would say, "OK, mother, it's time to start practicing so that when Thanksgiving and Christmas comes around, we will be ready." He would stand in the kitchen and taste the batter and say, "Not quite yet. Add a little *this*," or "It is missing a little *that*." When my mother had been around, I would let her taste the batter, and usually when she was there I would hit it right on the head. Woo-hoo my mother's pie!

I am not telling you that you can't have your mamma's sweet potatoes on this meal plan, but you can't eat them every day or even every week. You can have them twice a year, on Thanksgiving and Christmas. I know what you are saying: "*What?* You mean no candied yams every Sunday?" That's right, no candied yams every Sunday.

Let me explain: In addition to simple starches, sweet potatoes are rich in complex carbohydrates, dietary fiber, beta carotene (a vitamin A equivalent nutrient), vitamin C, and vitamin B6. The sweet potato, a root vegetable, is considered to have one of the highest nutritional values amongst all vegetables. Despite the name *sweet*, it can also be a beneficial food for diabetics, as it actually helps improve blood sugar. The irony is that we tend to add more sugar to the vegetable that God created to stabilize our blood sugar.

My family has a long history of diabetes—my father died from complications of diabetes, my mother had it, and four of my siblings are diabetic. I thanked God every day that I didn't develop diabetes, but I realized that without making changes in my lifestyle I would become the next member in the family to be crippled by the disease.

I began to talk with family members about their struggles with diabetes in an effort to educate myself on what *not* to do. My oldest sister has had Type II diabetes for nearly twenty years. She managed her diabetes through exercise, diet, regular testing of her blood levels, and taking prescribed medications. She shared with me that when she first discovered that she had diabetes, she started out by making minor changes to her daily life. She didn't change everything all at once; she took small steps to stay in balance. The key is to set goals you can reach. Here are the steps you can take, not all at the same time, but slowly adding each to your daily routine.

- Portion control
- Choose healthy carbohydrates
- Read nutrition labels
- Eat more often (consume six small meals a day, every three to four hours)
- Be consistent (eat the same number of meals each day, at the same time)
- Drink plenty of water
- Exercise (moderately)

My sister understood the importance of controlling her diabetes, and she wanted to make sure that diabetes didn't control her.

There are millions of people who are affected by diabetes. Many celebrities have come out of the closet about this disease. One famous person is the one and only Ms. Patti LaBelle. I love Ms. Patti not only because we are two girls from Philly, but also because she just keeps it real.

I have a copy of one of her cookbooks and discovered that she

too suffered from depression after she discovered she had diabetes. She tells the story of how she was faced with the decision
of giving the doctors permission to amputate both her mother's
legs and how diabetes took her mother from this world before
her time.[3]

Depression (or Patti's Pity Parties, the name her good friend
called them) kept her crying until she realized she had a pretty
terrific life. She began to recognize how blessed she was considering those that had passed in her family before her with dis-
eases that where not manageable like diabetes. So she stopped
focusing on the bad news of diabetes and started focusing on
the good news, that with the proper diet and exercise, you can
control this disease.[4]

I love Ms. Patti's story so much because once she understood
how to treat diabetes, she learned that it was not going on fad
diets like I did. She quickly understood, as she puts it, "Barbie
is a doll, not a goal....treat your body like a temple, not an
amusement park."[5] You can read her amazing story in her book
Patti LaBelle's Lite Cuisine. In there you will discover some
of the most delicious recipes that will warm your heart while
saving your life.

WHO IS MRS. DASH?

I love salt, so who is Mrs. Dash and why are we using it? I'm
sure you love a little bit of good gossip every now and then,
so I am going to feed that need and give you the scoop on
this Mrs. Dash. Ready? Mrs. Dash is Dietary Approaches to
Stop Hypertension, and part of the DASH low-sodium diet.
DASH...got it!

According to the 2010 Dietary Guidelines for Americans,
we should limit our sodium intake to less than 2,300 mg a

---

3   Patti LaBelle, with Laura Randolph Lancaster, *Patti LaBelle's Lite
Cuisine* (New York: Gotham Books, 2003).
4   Ibid.
5   Ibid., xxv.

day—1,500 mg if you're age fifty-one or older; if you're African American; or if you have high blood pressure, diabetes, or chronic kidney disease. Keep in mind that these are upper limits, and in this case less is better. If Mrs. Dash can help me lower my blood pressure and lose weight, I think she and I will be lifelong friends.

> What you choose to eat affects your chances of developing high blood pressure, also called hypertension. In an effort to help Americans reduce blood pressure, the Dietary Approaches to Stop Hypertension (DASH) diet is leading the way with the combination of an eating plan and reduced sodium intake. The DASH Diet approach to preventing hypertension presents a meal plan generous in fruits, vegetables, low-fat dairy, whole grains, poultry, fish, and nuts. It de-emphasizes fats, red meat, sweets, sodium, and sugar-containing beverages. The DASH Diet is low in total fat, saturated fat, and cholesterol, while high in potassium, calcium, magnesium, fiber and protein.
>
> Following the diet has been clinically proven to lower blood pressure. Here is a summary of the daily nutrient goals used in DASH studies (for a 2,100 calorie diet), along with tips to achieve these goals.[6]

Nutrient	Goal	Grocery List
Total Fat	27% of Calories	low or no fat dairy, poultry without skin (avoid dark meat), low or no fat salad dressings, spreads and condiments that add flavor without fat

---

6   "DASH Diet Fact Sheet," *Dietitian Center,* accessed March 30, 2013, http://www.dietitiancenter.com/userfiles/files/pdf/dash_diet-fact-sheet.pdf.

Nutrient	Goal	Grocery List
Saturated Fat	6% of Calories	vegetable oil spreads instead of butter, cook with olive or canola oil, choose lean cuts of meat and low or no fat dairy
Protein	18% of Calories	poultry, fish, nuts and beans
Carbohydrate	55% of Calories	whole grain breads, pastas, rice and cereals
Cholesterol	150 mg	lean meats, poultry, fish, low or no fat dairy
Sodium	2,300 mg	salt alternatives, spices, and avoid processed and canned foods
Potassium	4,700 mg	dried apricots, avocados, bananas, figs, kiwi, melon, beans, broccoli, carrots, Brussels sprouts, potatoes, winter squash, and spinach
Calcium	1,250 mg	milk, yogurt, cheese, and fortified foods and beverages
Magnesium	500 mg	artichokes, barley, oat bran, almonds, spinach and tomatoes
Fiber	30 g	pears, whole wheat pasta, whole grain cereals, lentils, black beans, lima beans, peas, and baked potato with skin

If you've been prescribed medications to lower your blood pressure, you need to keep taking those medications until your doctor is convinced you no longer need them. I once met a lady in her late twenties who said she tried to not use salt but found it difficult and that she wasn't going to take the medication that doctors prescribed her. I retorted, "You don't have to take the medication because dead people don't need meds."

Harsh, but true. She was overweight, in her late twenties, and on blood pressure medications—those medications may have been the only thing keeping her from an early death.

There is hope to reduce your blood pressure so that you don't have to continue taking medications, but once you've been prescribed the medication you must take it until a doctor says otherwise. Decreasing salt and increasing exercise are key factors to living a life free of blood pressure medication.

One day I went to the café at the job for lunch and decided on the low-calorie soup. By this time I had gotten in the habit of reading the nutrition labels on food items, and our café put nutrition labels on their foods. I gave it a quick glance. There were 985 mg of sodium per 6 ounces of soup—that's more than half my recommended daily amount! I was curious to see how many people would take the time to read the little labels over the soup pots. People came by and dipped the soup ladle without reading any of the nutritional value on the labels. After watching several people do this I stopped a lady before she poured her soup and asked her how much sodium she thought was in that 6-ounce cup of soup. She said she didn't know but proceeded to get a sample cup and try it out.

She said, "It doesn't taste salty."

I pointed out to her the sodium content on the label. She was shocked and didn't get the soup. She said it opened her eyes, and it was going to make her pay more attention to what was in her food before she put it in her body.

It's not just the salt we put on foods that we need to worry about. It's the salt already in foods that is a big concern. Read food labels! Here are a few tips on labels regarding sodium:

- No salt added: Salt has not been added during processing, but it may still have sodium.

- Reduced sodium: It contains at least 25 percent less sodium than the regular version of the food.

- Low-sodium: It contains 140 mg of sodium or less per serving.

- Very-low sodium: It contains 35 mg of sodium or less per serving.

- Sodium free: It contains less than 5 mg of sodium per serving.

TIPS TO SHAKE THE SALT HABIT WITHOUT SACRIFICING FLAVOR:

- When reducing salt in recipes, try using a no-salt seasoning, such as Mrs. Dash Salt-Free Seasoning Blends or Mr. Lee's Heavenly Seasonings.

- Add lemon juice or a splash of vinegar to vegetables, fish, and soups instead of salt.

- Instead of using soy sauce or salt in marinades, use herbs and spices, fruit juice, wine, flavored vinegars, or a ready-made salt-free marinade.

- Cook rice in low-sodium vegetable or chicken broth and add flavor with olive oil instead of butter. Then add onion, mushrooms, celery, and herbs.

- Reduce the salt content of canned foods by draining and rinsing the food before cooking.

HEAVENLY SEASONINGS

Now I would like you to meet a very good friend of mine named Lee Armstrong—or Mr. Lee, as I like to call him. As long as I have known Lee and his beautiful wife, Denise, he has been on a quest to develop healthy dishes. Years ago he became aware that something had to be done in their household when he discovered his wife was extremely sensitive to the food additive MSG. Her optometrist verified that MSG was the source of migraine headaches Denise had been experiencing on more than one occasion, which caused temporary blindness.

The choices that were afforded to him during that time were not very palatable, so he went on a four-year journey with food scientists and spice manufacturers to create unique spice blends with intense flavors without salt or sugar. Dear God, what a labor of love. He has now packaged these spices in several blends after a friend tasted them and said, "Lee, these spices are simply heavenly"—hence the birth of Heavenly Seasonings.

They are seven years in the making, with a proprietary formula being produced by one of the top spice houses in America. His products are the next generation of spices that are Kosher certified and exceed all USDA requirements.

Mr. Lee is now testing his Heavenly Seasonings in hospital cafeterias throughout the country. God knows we need some good food in hospitals. At this time he has developed several spices that are available on his website, www.heavenlyseasonings.com.

I have tried all of these spices and they are very good. My favorites are:

- *The Classic Blend*, which also comes in hot, mild, and mesquite smoke flavors. I have added this seasoning to chicken and my son Ronald's classic kale chips. They give barbeque potato chips a run for their money. (You can find Ronald's Classic Kale Chips recipe at the end of this section.)

- *The Seafood Boil*, a unique, snappy boil that is positioned for all seafood lovers, including those on restrictive diets. Available in hot and mild, I use this on my famous grilled salmon that always keeps my family asking if there's any salmon left. It is also great on crab legs and shrimp.

- *Honey Butter Garlic Dill*—just that name should get your mouth watering. Use this as a marinade on salmon, steamed, broiled or baked potatoes or in potato salad. This is also great on corn, cauliflower, peas, and carrots, and my favorite sweet potatoes.

Here are a few of Mr. Lee's famous recipes:

LEE'S SLAMMING SALMON

Ingredients:

Salmon fillets

Heavenly Seasonings' Honey Butter Garlic Dill

Fresh lemon or lime juice

Directions (do ahead):

Clean and pat dry fillets
   Squeeze lemon or lime juice over fillets
   Coat with Honey Butter Garlic Dill
   Place in dish and refrigerate overnight

Fish can be grilled, sautéed, or baked (at 350 degrees for 7–10 minutes) to your desired doneness.

HEAVENLY CAULIFLOWER

Ingredients:

1 large head of cauliflower (per 3 people)

Heavenly Seasonings' Honey Butter Garlic Dill

½ cup plain Greek yogurt

2 Tbsp. chives

8 oz extra sharp white cheddar cheese, shredded

2 Tbsp. butter

Directions:

Break cauliflower head down to florets and place in a steamer pan (do not boil)

Generously sprinkle with Heavenly Seasonings' Honey Butter Garlic Dill before cooking

Steam until fork tender, remove and place in mixing bowl. Sprinkle 2 Tbsp. Honey Butter Garlic Dill over in bowl

Add butter, Greek yogurt, cheddar cheese, and chives, and mix until lumpy like smashed potatoes. (In fact, you can use a potato smasher instead of a mixer if desired.)

Enjoy!

SUPER HEALTHY QUINOA

Ingredients:

1 cup quinoa

2 cups chicken stock

¼ cup chopped onions (Vidalia or red)

¼ cup red bell peppers

¼ cup yellow bell peppers

¼ cup orange bell peppers

½ cup corn (fresh or frozen)

½ cup green peas (fresh or frozen)

¼ cup Craisins or raisins

2–3 slices turkey bacon, sliver sliced

½ cup butternut squash, finely cubed (or cubed carrots)

3 Tbsp. olive oil

2 Tbsp. Heavenly Seasonings' Classic Blend or Mesquite Blend (hot or mild, to taste)

[3-qt. saucepan]

Directions:

In a 3-quart saucepan, place 3 Tbsp. olive oil, heat.

Fry bacon strips (cross cut bacon ¼ wide) to done.

Add chicken stock, Craisins or raisins, onion, and Heavenly Seasonings' Classic Blend or Mesquite, and bring to a boil.

Add to boiling liquid all remaining veggies and quinoa, let return to a boil

Reduce temp to a simmer, cover and let simmer for 15–20 minutes. When done, it will resemble a pot of correctly cooked rice.

Use as a side dish, or bedding for meats. Enjoy!

Heavenly Slow Cooked Chicken

Ingredients:

½–1 chicken cut-up (or the parts you prefer)

3 celery stalks

1 vidalia onion

1–2 bell peppers (colors of choice)

1 cup mushrooms

2 rutabagas (or 3 potatoes, if you are not diabetic)

1 can of low-salt cream of mushroom soup

Heavenly Seasonings' Honey Butter Garlic Dill (for a mild, subtle flavor profile); Heavenly Seasonings' Classic Blend or Mesquite Blend (hot or mild, to taste)

[4-quart slow cooker or Crock Pot]

Directions:

Clean and season chicken. Set aside.

Clean and cube up rutabagas or potatoes

Thick-slice mushrooms, onions, bell peppers, and celery stalks.

Place ingredients into slow cooker in the following order:
    1. Rutabagas or potatoes on the bottom
    2. First layer of all veggies
    3. Sprinkle generously with Heavenly Seasonings of choice
    4. Layer of chicken

5. Second layer of all veggies

6. Next layer of chicken, if necessary

7. Top layer of veggies and cream of mushroom soup

8. Top coat of generous sprinkling of Heavenly Seasonings

Turn slow cooker on low either the night before, or turn on when leaving for work. Awaken or return home to your home full of the delectable aroma! Enjoy.

BEST EVER GRANDMA VIOLA'S TOMATO SOUP

Ingredients:

1 64 oz can of low-salt tomato juice

¼ cup olive oil

½ gallon of plain almond of soy milk (your choice)

2 large Vidalia onions

¾ cup flour

¼ stick butter (to your taste and health restrictions)

Heavenly Seasonings California Garlic Pepper, or Heavenly Seasonings Classic Blend, or Mesquite Blend (hot or mild, to taste)

[3-qt. saucepan]

[6-qt. saucepan]

Directions:

Put tomato juice in 3-qt. saucepan on medium heat, bring to simmer

Put olive oil in 6-qt. saucepan, slice onions and sauté until translucent

Add generous amount (2–3 Tbsp.) of Heavenly Seasonings to onions

Add flour to onion, stirring. Make a roux.

Add milk to roux, stirring (can use a whisk). Bring to a simmer.

Add butter.

(IMPORTANT: In this order.) Add hot tomato juice to milk mixture. (If you reverse, it will curdle.) Stir in thoroughly.

If you have a hand processor, blend up onions finely in pot; if not, you can strain onions out of soup, add puree in food processor or blender, and reintroduce to soup.

This will be the absolute best (and healthiest) tomato soup you have ever tasted!

KALE

My son Ronald really loves eating healthy. I can remember when he came home from school one day and told me he was no longer going to eat pork or beef. My thought to him was, child, you will eat whatever I cook and put on this table. Who do you think you are, telling me you don't eat pork of beef? Out of the mouths of babes, right? Maybe if I had paid attention to him back in the day when he told me this, I would have had better eating habits.

Fast forward to today and this kid—or should I say, young man—is still eating healthy. One day I went to the store and he asked me to pick up some kale chips. When I got home and gave them to him, he opened the bag and grabbed a handful and began to eat them. Shortly after he called me and said, "Mom, I just read the label and these chips have cashews in them. I'm getting sick." Ronald has very bad allergies to cashews. That $3.00 bag of chips cost me over $200.00 with the doctor visit and prescription meds because we didn't read the label.

That didn't stop Ronald from desiring kale chips, because kale is what we call a superstar vegetable. When I was young we ate a lot of collards and now my family loves to eat kale. I make raw kale salad, which they love, besides Ronald's kale chips.

According to Wikipedia, "Kale is very high in beta carotene, vitamin K, vitamin C, and rich in calcium. Kale is a source of two carotenoids, lutein and zeaxanthin. Kale, as with broccoli and other brassicas, contains sulforaphane (particularly when chopped or minced), a chemical with potent anti-cancer properties. Boiling decreases the level of sulforaphane; however, steaming, microwaving, or stir frying do not result in significant loss. Along with other brassica vegetables, kale is also a source of indole-3-carbinol, a chemical which boosts DNA repair in cells and appears to block the growth of cancer cells. Kale has been found to contain a group of resins known as bile acid sequestrants, which have been shown to lower cholesterol and decrease absorption of dietary fat."[7]

RONALD'S KALE CHIPS

Ingredients:

A bunch of kale

1 Tbsp. extra virgin olive oil

Heavenly Seasonings' Classic Blend Mesquite

---

7   *Wikipedia*, s.v. "Kale", http://en.wikipedia.org/wiki/Kale (accessed June 11, 2013).

Sea salt to taste (optional)

Directions:

Wash a bundle of kale. (I like the curly-leaf kale, but any will do.)

Place kale flat on a cookie sheet, and pat dry with a paper towel.

Add 1 Tbsp. of extra virgin olive oil over the leaves.

Place in a preheated oven at 300 degrees for 15–20 minutes or until leaves are crispy. (Time varies based on ovens.)

Add Heavenly Seasonings Classic Blend Mesquite.

Add sea salt to taste if you want, and enjoy.

LYNETTE'S FAMOUS KALE SALAD

Ingredients:

1–2 fresh kale bunches (or a bag of chopped kale)

1 clove fresh garlic, chopped

2 Tbsp. olive oil

½ red onion

Sea salt (to taste)

2 Tbsp. natural yeast

Directions:

Wash the bundles of kale.

In a medium bowl, add kale, olive oil, ½ chopped red onion, garlic, sea salt, and yeast.

Combine all ingredients, and add chopped grilled chicken or steamed or grilled shrimp to make this salad a meal. Enjoy!

Chapter Seven

FILLED WITH ORGANIZATION

A S I BEGAN my transformation, I needed a way to keep up with all the changes. I had to get organized and develop some routines. My life had been turned upside-down over the last few years, and I was ridiculously unorganized as a result. I knew that if I were going to be successful in changing my eating and exercise habits I would have to change some lifestyle habits and be disciplined about it all.

In order to ensure that I was eating healthy foods I decided that I needed to cook my foods and bring my lunch to work. In order to cook, I had to shop. And in order to shop, I had to schedule time for the grocery store during my weekend. Before my transformation, during the weekends I would sleep late, hang out with friends and family, and take myself to the movies or out to eat. While there is nothing wrong with any of those activities, the new me had to set aside time on the weekends to prepare for the next week. I started making preparations a priority, and social activities became secondary.

I would try to prepare enough food to eat for dinner during the week so that I didn't have to eat late when I came home from work. I found that it was helpful to plan my meals for the week and do my grocery shopping Saturday morning before the grocery store was crowded. I also purchased a steamer, which has become another best friend (by this time I had replaced Perky with several new friends). I would steam, sauté, bake, or broil my meats and vegetables then divide my meals up into several plastic containers for lunch and dinner.

If you have children and you work late, this is a great way for them to eat a balanced meal. If you have cooked for the week, just pull out a dinner from the freezer, microwave, and sit with your family for a nice, home-cooked meal.

These are just a few things that I have done in order to stay organized and commit to eating a well-balanced meal each day. It has also kept me from paying for breakfast or lunch during work days, which saved a considerable amount of money. I calculated all the money I spent on breakfast and lunch during the weeks, months, and year, and the amount was shocking. On average, I spent seventy-five dollars per week, three hundred dollars per month, and thirty-six hundred dollars per year—not including evenings and weekends when I ate out at restaurants or fast-food joints.

Spending half of my Saturday each week to prepare my food for the week has saved me well over four thousand dollars a year. Not only can a healthy lifestyle provide a spiritual, mental, and physical transformation, but when your life comes back into focus you may experience a financial transformation as well. I took the money I was saving and started paying off my credit cards. First lose the weight and then lose the debt.

As I began finding a sense of calm and serenity in becoming organized, I decided to declutter more areas of my life. As a result of my weight loss all my old clothes no longer fit. I donated most of them, and the rest I took to a consignment shop. I stopped going to the malls to shop because I was not finished losing weight. I promised myself a new wardrobe when I reached my goal weight. Until then, I would wear what I had and have fun with accessories. The more organized I became the more centered and relaxed I felt.

I didn't become an unorganized mess overnight, just like I

didn't wake up one morning suddenly overweight. Like losing weight, getting organized takes time and discipline. Keep it simple. Make one change at a time and seek help if you need it. Don't try to do it all in one day.

In addition to getting my daily life organized, I decided it was time to organize my future focus. I created a vision board. A vision board is a simple tool to help you manifest the things you want most in life. Use a poster board and create a collage of images and writings from magazines or the Internet that project who you want to become, what you want to have, where you want to live, or even where you want to vacation. Then make life changes to match those images and desires. Put all your dreams on the vision board and keep it in a place where you will see it daily. Make the desires pictured on your vision board a priority in your life. Ask yourself if your list brings value and positive impact to your life. For some of you it may be money, health, business, or family goals. For me it was a healthy spiritual, physical, and mental balance. I knew that once those things were aligned in my life everything else would fall into place.

If your desires on your vision board don't move you toward your ultimate life goals, then eliminate them. Eliminate low-value tasks to free up more time for the things that are most important to you. Evaluate your life and focus on the things that provide the most value. Remember, tomorrow is never promised, so get the most out of your life today.

Chapter Eight

FILLED WITH EXERCISE

HOW MANY TIMES have you heard or said, "If I had a trainer, I could I lose weight," or "If I had a personal chef, I would eat right." I was guilty of saying that too. More so, I *believed* that was the only way I could lose weight. I don't think that way anymore. Trainers, gyms, personal chefs, and weight-loss plans don't work.

Hold on! Before you put the book down and call me crazy, let me explain. Oprah had a trainer—the famous Bob Greene. She also had a personal chef, she went to the gym, she even had a gym built at her studio (and probably her home too). But look at what happened: she gained all that weight back. Don't get me wrong. I have much love and respect for the Queen of Talk and hope to meet her one day to talk about this very book—but today I'll use her to prove a point. I'm sure she would agree: it's not the gym or the trainer or the chef that makes you successful at losing weight. The only thing that can guarantee success is *you* making a decision and then managing the decision you make.

Once I made the decision that I wanted to lose weight, 90 percent of the work was done. The other 10 percent was getting my big butt up and out of the bed and getting to the gym. That's my 90/10 rule. Weight loss is 90 percent mental. I had to free my mind of doubt and excuses and complaints, and then the other 10 percent followed.

How many people do you know who join a gym every year as their New Year's resolution? Why do we fail by February? Why does it seem so hard to stay on board with our commitments? It's because we lack the ability to manage ourselves. I am a great manager at work, home, church, and even in my family. But I failed to invest in and manage *me*.

Then my revelations came, and I wanted to lose weight, not for a man, not to fit into a dress, not to attend an event, not for vanity, but for myself. If there was anyone else that I lost weight for, it was my children. I wanted to live to see my grandkids. I wanted to be healthy. I thought about all the medications my mother had been taking before she died, and I found the motivation to go to the gym and get moving.

So if you can't afford Bob Greene, here are some tricks to get you moving:

- Get up and walk every day—it doesn't cost you a gym membership for that!
- Get that bike out of the garage and get on it.
- Join the YMCA or your local gym.
- Find workout classes or dance classes that you enjoy.
- Purchase a fun workout video and work out at home.
- Purchase exercise bands.
- Purchase some weights.
- Try something new like inline skating.
- Try something old like roller-skating.

- Dance. I love to put on salsa music and clean the house.

- Swim or start water aerobics classes—check your county or city aquatic center.

- Take your kids ice-skating.

- Have fun with Wii Fit and Wii Active games, or games on the Xbox Kinect.

- Play tennis with friends at your community court.

- Participate in cycling rides with teams and clubs.

By doing some of these things I had finally broken the "I don't feel like getting up and working out" spirit. You know that spirit that gets in the bed with you and lays on you and holds you down so you don't get up, the one that talks you into staying up late the night before so that you are too tired to get up, or the one that makes you have a bad day *every* day just so that you will not go to the gym after work? Yeah, that one. That spirit comes in all shapes and sizes to distract you. It will come looking like your kids, your spouse, your family, your job, your boss, your coworkers, and it will also come looking like *you*.

One day I realized that my inner procrastinator wasn't just making me fat and lazy; it was trying to kill me. I have a history of heart disease, high blood pressure, and diabetes in my family. Being overweight and not exercising were setting me up for an early grave. When I had gotten sick on the cruise I had been scared. I knew if I was experiencing high blood pressure I was on my way to having diabetes and this combination could easily lead to stroke and death.

I knew I had to get beyond the excuses and move toward results. Although it sat collecting dust for a while, the Wii Fit game my son got me for my birthday ended up being the perfect start to an exercise routine, and I didn't even need a gym membership. The game had aerobics, yoga, and several other games to get my heart rate up and get me fit. I was so motivated by the game that I also got Wii Active. This takes your fitness to the next level. The game even has a personal trainer that can tell when you are slacking off during exercise. It maps out your exercise program based on your fitness goals, just like a real trainer, and you can track your progress.

Once I got in the habit of being active, I decided to take a spin class at my gym. *Spin* is a class where you ride stationary bikes with an instructor guiding you up and down imaginary hills as you switch gears, all to the sound of music. It's a great way to burn calories and strengthen leg muscles, such as the quads, hamstrings, and calves. It also helps to lift, tighten, and develop those butt muscles. Spin class was essential to my weight loss.

When I climb on that bike I zone out and let my mind take me to places that have rolling hills and beautiful mountains. One day during spin class the instructor mentioned organized rides for charitable causes. He said that there are several of them throughout the year and in different locations in the city. It was time to take my bike on the road.

I signed up for my first ride, and it was to benefit research for multiple sclerosis (MS). I didn't know anyone with the disease, but I was aware that it was a potentially debilitating disease that attacked the nervous system and could eventually lead to a complete inability to control your bodily functions—things as simple as walking and talking. I was proud to ride for the cause.

On these rides you meet all kinds of people, and complete strangers become friends. I met one lady who stopped with me at a resting point. She told me that this would be her last stop; she had to end the ride early because her body was getting very tired. I thought to myself I was tired too, but I didn't say it aloud. Thank goodness I didn't, because she then proceeded to tell me that she had MS. We had already completed fifty miles by that point, and if she hadn't told me I never would have known that her body was stricken with the disease. I got my tired, sore tail back on that bike that day and finished the ride for her. I didn't know her name, but I completed sixty-five miles and crossed the finish line for her and all the others who can't ride for themselves.

When I was approached about fundraising and riding in the 2009 Tour De Cure for Diabetes, I didn't think twice. I had never understood how crippling diabetes could be until I took care of my mother and had to check her blood sugar twice a day and give her insulin shots to regulate it. Although my father died of complications from diabetes and my sisters and brother have this disease, I wasn't aware how serious the disease was until I took care of mother. I hate needles, and I couldn't imagine having to give myself shots every day, sometimes twice a day, for the rest of my life. Instead, I lost the weight that threatened to bring me diabetes, and I rode in the Tour De Cure for Diabetes to honor all those who suffer from the disease.

SUMMARY

The 90/10 rule is simple. Diets, gym membership, and trainers don't work if you don't work. Your weight loss is truly mental. When I started my weight loss quest I began without a trainer. It was important for me to depend on my own ability, as I had failed with trainers before. Once I was confident that I was committed to my health and had lost a significant amount of weight on my own, I did hire a trainer to help with strength training and take me to that next level of fitness. One of the first things he did was to explain the body's anatomy.

Don't get me wrong, I have seen the human anatomy before, but never in the mindset of muscle structure and how it relates to my training. He showed me how God designed our bodies to be—which is not with fat covering our muscles. He showed me pictures of some of the world's greatest body builders and how their bodies looked just like the anatomy pictures. He went on to say that God had created the skin as protection, and if we could zip the skin off of these body builders we would see what was in the anatomy books. I was fascinated with the body structure and how it was made up.

My trainer started training my mind before he ever had me pick up a weight or do a sit-up. My trainer was the 90/10 rule in action. Here are a few more lessons he shared with me:

- When selecting foods or activities, you are always in control.

- When eating in a restaurant that may not be as healthy as you would like, tell the server that you are on a special eating plan and ask them if they can make a few modifications or changes.

- Read labels and reduce the fat in your house as well as in your body. This was a big lesson I learned when he came to my house and did a surprise sweep of the kitchen.

- Proper breathing during exercising will sustain you. He would always say, "Your breath will carry you there."

- Keep a food journal of what you eat each day.

- Learn to take time out at the end of the workout to stretch and be quiet. Meditate and let your mind go to a peaceful place before jumping back into the world.

- Drink plenty of water and drink a good protein drink right after working out.

- Meditate on your overall fitness goals and envision the new you.

- Make a daily affirmation that you are healthy.

- Write your fitness goals down and keep them before you at all times.

Chapter Nine

FILLED WITH SUPPORT

A S I BEGAN the Lynette Jackson makeover, obstacles and distractions came often. As I was trying to lose weight, my old friend food called upon me often. In my old job we had "Bagel Thursday." To boost employee morale (and waistlines) our division bought bagels, muffins, and sweet breads for the entire staff. In my role I managed many of the day-to-day operations of our department. One of the things that I was responsible for was the ordering and distribution of— you guessed it—the bagels, muffins, and sweet breads for Bagel Thursday.

When we started this token of appreciation for our staff I was in the middle of my second week of my new eating plan. Each week I was tortured by the delicious aroma of fresh baked bagels and the flavored cream cheeses. The smell of toasted bagels wafted from the break room, and I knew I was being tested. I gave myself a "cheat day" with my eating once a week, but I reserved that for Sundays. I just couldn't waste a cheat day on a stupid bagel or muffin.

I needed help. How could I manage a Thursday without sneaking a piece of bagel? I decided to ask a coworker for her support. She agreed to put out the bagels for me so I wouldn't have to see or touch the temptation. I was lucky to find someone who was so supportive. She came in early each week to handle both our bagel duties, and she was happy to support me in my goals.

But I learned that you can't always trust people to be supportive of you when you are trying to do something good for yourself. Oftentimes people don't know how to be supportive, and other times they are jealous of your achievements. When you share your thoughts and dreams with people and they find all the things wrong with what you are doing or they laugh or say negative things to you, you should step back and realize that you are dealing with a dream stealer. Once you're aware of this type of person, they can never steal your dreams again.

Sometimes these dream-stealers will steal your ideas, and sometimes when they're closest to you these people will steal the dreams right out of your heart. I used to let people take my dreams from me. I remember once someone close to me said, "We know that you aren't bragging about stuff, because you don't really have any stuff to brag about, but you're always upbeat about what you are doing or where you are going." I was a little hurt by that comment. If I can't share my life with my friends and family, who can I tell? If I can't talk about how excited I am about the wonderful things that are happening to me with my loved ones, then who will share in my joy? I realized that some people will try to discourage you at your greatest moments in life. They are dream stealers, and they are not the type of support that you need when you are working diligently to change your life for the better.

It is important, especially during this time in your life, to find support from people that have like minds and goals. You may have to distance yourself from some of your old friends and develop relationships with new friends. Get rid of the haters and the naysayers. If anything, use their hate to motivate—let their doubts be the very fuel to motivate you to fulfill your dreams.

As I lost weight I had to let go of some close friends who were happier to see me overweight and killing myself than healthy and happy. Misery loves company, and I wasn't miserable any longer. It was hard to say good-bye to some good friends, but when I realized that they were going to pull and tear me down I was quick to let them go. One person said to me, quite sarcastically, "You are just so happy about your weight loss." Well, shouldn't I be happy about my weight loss? I actually had people stop speaking to me or hanging out with me because I was able to accomplish something that they wanted to do but hadn't been able to complete. I am looking for the type of friend who will say, "I thank God that you lost that weight and can live a happy and healthy life. I'm proud of you and happy for you." If you have friends who don't bring joy to you, then they don't need to be in your life. Surround yourself with positive people, and they will help you reach your goals.

I found a wonderful support group when I decided to try something new and learn to scuba dive. In March 2009 I saw an advertisement for a scuba class at my health club. Ever since I had taken an introductory scuba course at a resort in Barbados years ago I had wanted to get scuba certified.

As a child I went to the neighborhood pool in Philadelphia and splashed around to cool off on a hot summer day. As an adult I loved to vacation on a beach with blue water. When I moved to Florida I rented a house with a pool. Despite my love for water, I had some deep-rooted fears that I wanted to eliminate.

Without hesitation, I signed up for scuba orientation at the health club. I met one of my greatest supporters, Jim Consuegra, the best scuba teacher in the world. Jim went over the course requirements, but all I heard was that the PADI (Professional Association of Diving Instructors) course required we swim two hundred meters nonstop in order to be certified. Two hundred meters without stopping? That's four laps in an Olympic-size swimming pool and eight laps in the twenty-five-meter pool we would be using! What was I thinking?

Jim went around the class and asked each of us why we had decided to take the scuba class. When my turn came I admitted that I had a fear of deep water, and I wanted to face it. He gave us lots of information about what would take place during the course and the safety precautions we would need to take as we began to dive. All of a sudden I remembered why I had a fear of deep water, and I began asking lots of questions.

"What about sharks?"

"Do fish bite?"

"What other sea animals will we see?"

Somehow it never dawned on me to ask Jim what type of physical shape I needed to be in to scuba dive. Orientation was coming to a close, and I had to make the decision whether or not I wanted to pay the full price and get certified.

"Are you in, Lynette?" Jim asked.

"OK, I'm in."

It didn't seem like it would be that hard. Little did I know that it would be the hardest thing I had ever done. But in the process I would learn valuable lessons about support and commitment.

On the first day of class I was sick at home nursing a sinus infection. I knew my dedication was being tested, but I couldn't attend class no matter how much I wanted. By the second day of class I was back at work and ready for the challenge. While scuba sounded fun and exciting, I was about to discover that the physical aspect of the class was more challenging than I ever could have imagined.

The most surprising discovery I made was that I couldn't swim. The swimming I had been doing, apparently, was not swimming—it was playing in the water. I couldn't swim ten meters, let alone two hundred! A few great swimmers in the class passed the test that first night we got in the pool. I was a long way from two hundred meters; just one hundred and ninety meters to go.

I wasn't the only one struggling to swim, though; there was

a young man named Paul and a woman about my age named Sherry who, like me, opted out of testing on the two hundred meters each week. Jim would begin each class asking if anyone wanted to test, and each week someone other than the three of us would volunteer to swim the seemingly impossible two hundred meters. I was practicing, but my progress was so slow that I'd be in a retirement home before I passed the test. Then one day, Paul said, "I am tired of not testing. I am going to take some swimming classes so that I can get this done."

And he did. After a few more classes Paul tested and passed.

Each week we had to swim to warm up before class. Each week Sherry and I were the last two out of the pool. We were slow to realize that it wasn't just our technique that was pathetic; we weren't in the physical condition to pass the test. When we swam we would put our head down under water, but as soon as we got tired, our heads would pop out of the water like turtles. We excelled in the other aspects of training for the scuba certi-fication: we could handle our equipment, clear our mask under water, retrieve our regulators, and deal with all the other exer-cises that we would be required to perform for certification. We just couldn't swim.

My inability to swim was becoming such a hindrance that I was beginning to dread going to class. I left class each week wondering, *Why am I putting myself through this? I don't need to prove anything to anyone. Just quit. Sigh, I am getting too old for this.* But somehow I wouldn't give in to my doubts, because the very next week I would be back in class trying again. Of course, I can't take all the credit for not listening to my inner critic. Sherry wouldn't let me quit, and she e-mailed or called me often to keep me encouraged. Paul would also reassure me and boost my spirits. "You can do this. Just keep your head down," he would say. He'd often send me an e-mail reminding me that I just needed to believe in myself. Little did Paul and Sherry know how much I needed their words of inspiration. If I didn't swim the two hundred meters, I couldn't get certified. If

I couldn't get certified, I'd have wasted hundreds of dollars on the course and the trip to Bimini, Bahamas, for our open-water certification.

At the end of the last class, as everyone was getting out of the pool, Jim said, "Lynette and Sherry, I need you in the water."

My heart stopped. I wasn't ready. I knew everything else we had learned would have been in vain if we didn't pass this test. Still, I wasn't ready; neither was Sherry.

We eased ourselves back in the pool and began to swim. Despite our best efforts, we both failed to complete the two hundred meters. I wasn't even close. I was about one hundred meters short of passing the test. We both felt defeated, and I feared what Jim would say next, but he was kind. "You girls have put up a good try and a good fight. Here's what I am going to do. We are not scheduled to leave for Bimini until June 30. It is now the end of April. I will let you take the swimming test sometime between now and then. Take some classes and get in the water each week. You will improve, but when I call for you to swim, there will be no more excuses. I want my two hundred, and that's that!"

I left the pool that night still feeling defeated despite Jim's good intentions, and regardless of the extra time we were granted I wanted to quit. I was forty-seven years young, but every muscle in my body was hurting. I had never done anything so physically grueling, and I wasn't excited about the extra time; I just wanted to quit.

But good old Sherry wouldn't let me give up. "We are in this thing to win it and go to Bimini and dive."

Jim was an angel, checking on us weekly via e-mail, text, or Facebook. He would ask, "Are you swimming, my little swim girls?" Admittedly, I didn't start my lessons right away because I was still contemplating throwing in the towel. Sherry was already swimming at the YMCA near her house, and eventually I relented and decided to call the local aquatic center in my county. I talked with a coach named Judy and told her my dilemma. She agreed to help me and told me that if I was willing to train with her twice a week she could have me swimming by my next test in one month.

I accepted her challenge and committed to swim lessons on Thursday evenings and Saturday mornings. I had just completed six weeks of grueling physical activity in the pool for the scuba lessons, and now, as a black woman, I was going to be getting my hair wet twice a week for the next four weeks. I must have been insane.

Thursday arrived, and I headed to the pool. Coach Judy had told me she was the coach of a swim team called the Tara Tarpons, and they would be practicing that same day. What she didn't tell me was that the Tarpons were a bunch of kids no more than ten years old. They were jumping off the diving board and doing every swim stroke imaginable in twelve-feet-deep water. I was a bit intimidated—by elementary school kids!

Coach Judy told me to go to the locker room, change, and meet her at the shallow end of the pool. I wanted to leave, and I already had no intentions of coming back to be embarrassed by a bunch of snotty-nosed brats. But for the moment I swallowed my pride and eased into the shallow end of the pool. Coach Judy asked me to swim the width of the pool so she could see my form. She watched me swim awkwardly to the other side and immediately began to teach me drills.

Our first drill was reminiscent of something you'd teach a toddler. She had me stand in the pool with my face in the water and blow bubbles. Was she kidding? I was forty-seven-years old, five feet nine inches tall, and standing in three feet of water blowing bubbles. I couldn't imagine how this would help me reach my goal within a month.

Sherry called me later to find out how I had enjoyed my swimming lessons. I told her how humiliated I felt but admitted that I sensed Coach Judy had some grand scheme that might work. I decided to go back on Saturday. I went every Thursday night and every Saturday morning.

Then the dreaded call came from Jim. "Hello, my little swim girls. Are you ready to swim for me?"

Although I had gotten significantly better and had drastically increased my endurance, I still couldn't complete the entire two hundred meters without pausing. Still, Jim insisted we take the test. Sherry and I were nervous; this was the make it or break it moment. We hit the water and swam for our lives. My heart was pounding so hard and so fast that about fifty meters from my finish I got so caught up in my heartbeat that I lost my focus. We were swimming in twelve feet of water, and as my stroke became slower and off rhythm I began sinking. I fought hard to gain my momentum back, but eventually I had to grab on to the side of the pool. I had failed.

Sherry's nervousness overpowered her too, and she also psyched herself out of completing the test. We got out of the pool, and I couldn't stop the tears from flowing down my face. I had given up hours and hours of my time and energy learning to swim. I had gotten my hair wet twice a week, and for what?

Jim called us both to sit down. He told us how proud he was that we had never quit. Each week when he thought we wouldn't show up, we did. He then explained that the two hundred meters *non-stop* was a "Jim-ism" and that PADI only required we swim two hundred meters *total*. Apparently we swam that far in one of our first few water lessons. Jim had insisted on the additional requirement as his own safety measure, but it didn't prevent us from passing the PADI course.

I was furious with Jim. I wanted to throw him in the pool where Sherry and I could hold him down and drown him.

"You mean to tell me that we passed a long time ago?"

"Yes."

"So why did you make us keep swimming?"

"Because you could swim but you were not great swimmers. I knew if I didn't push you, you would only be OK swimmers. Now you are swimming one thousand times better than your first night."

I wiped away the tears and allowed myself to quietly celebrate this truth. Not only had I passed the test, but I was a *much* better swimmer. The open ocean is no joke, and swimming better would only help me. OK, Jim wasn't such a bad guy after all. But he did still insist that we take the test once more to try and reach his goal of two hundred meters before our trip. It wouldn't stop us from going on the trip if we didn't pass; it would just be our gift to him for working with us and not failing us at the end of the course. He said that he was going to host a "Get Wet" refresher course right before we left for our certification trip to Bimini and that we needed to keep swimming until then.

The night of the "Get Wet" refresher I was still nervous about passing that test. Jim was so busy getting all of our scuba gear ready to take overseas to Bimini for our certification trip that I hoped he wouldn't remember our test. The class went through the refresher course, and everyone was getting out of the pool when I heard Jim say, "Sherry and Lynette, I want you to give me my two hundred tonight. You didn't forget that you were going to swim for me, did you?"

The nervous feeling crept into my stomach as usual, but Sherry and I just looked at each other and decided to give it our all. We jumped back into the pool, took a good breath, kept our heads down, and paced ourselves. I felt like Michael Phelps in the water. I probably didn't look like Phelps, but I sure felt like I was an Olympic swimmer that night. I could see Jim's feet walking on the side of the pool back and forth as we swam. I had started so quickly that I started getting winded about fifteen meters from the finish. I could hear my breathing change, and Jim later told me that he could see my body language change.

The whole time he was yelling, "You are fifteen meters away. Don't you quit on me! Don't you quit! You keep swimming! Swim! Swim! Swim! Do not quit! You are almost there!"

When I looked up, I was approaching the wall, and then I hit it. I had accomplished my most difficult challenge.

Sherry was right behind me. We passed! We were exhausted but giddy with excitement and pride. As we got out of the pool we slapped each other high five. These two non-swimmers just swam two hundred meters.

We arrived in Bimini on a beautiful Wednesday morning. After checking into our hotel we had lunch and then reported to the boat to take our first dive. I couldn't believe that the next time I put on my gear I would be jumping into the ocean instead of a pool. I was going scuba diving.

All those weeks of scuba training and swim lessons were finally about to pay off, and I was going to get my open-water certification. I was anxious, and when Jim asked us what our apprehension rate was on a scale of one to ten, I blurted out, "An eight!"

The boat took us away from land, and the open ocean was before us. The water was blue, but the sea was rough. The boat was rocking up and down and side to side so hard that I thought we were going to fall over. It was hard to walk around or even move. I began to feel sick. Jim had said that we might get a little seasick, but I thought, *If the seas are rough, shouldn't we just wait until it calms down and do this tomorrow?* Jim must have sensed my fear, because he assured us that once we got in the ocean and began to descend the sea would calm. However, by now Sherry and I were both getting sick. The rocking only got worse, and eventually I found myself with my head hanging over the side of the boat giving my lunch to the fish in the sea. I was miserable.

The seas were so rough that we had to enter the ocean in a seated position from the back of the boat. We had always practiced the giant stride where you walk straight off the side of the boat. Now I was sick and nervous and scared.

"Let's go, Lynette. Off you go."

I said a quick prayer and into the water I went. *This isn't so bad*, I thought. But the waves quickly started throwing us around again, and I couldn't wait to get underwater, where I was told it was calmer. Once everyone got in, Jim gave us the signal to descend and we did. Finally.

My boss, who was a PADI diver, had been so proud of me for completing the course in the face of all my obstacles that he had given me a dive computer, which looks like a digital watch with a big face. I looked at the computer as we slowly descended. Twenty feet. Thirty feet. Forty feet. Fifty feet. There I was, fifty feet below the ocean's surface—and it was the most beautiful sight I had ever seen. We lay on the ocean floor, and I noticed the comforting calm that surrounded me. For forty-five minutes we explored the bottom of the ocean with its colorful array of fish and sea creatures.

I wanted to stay longer, but it was time to go back to the surface. We were about ten feet from the surface when I felt the water get choppy again, and then I started feeling sick. By the time I got on the boat I had to run to the side, where I fed the fish the remainder of my lunch and most of my breakfast. I was so sick, but we had to do another dive. Jim paired me with Sherry for the next dive, which was a twenty-five-foot dive.

We were always paired with a buddy. Sherry and I had already been through so much together that it seemed only natural for her to be my scuba buddy. Jim had always said that scuba diving could really be taught in a lesson or two, but the six weeks of intense training was mainly about what to do in case of an emergency. I was trained to save Sherry's life, and she was trained to save mine.

Scuba taught me a very valuable lesson: we all need support. My "lone ranger" mentality was coming to an end, and I was learning the value in having a buddy—someone who had my back. We were trained never to let our buddy out of our sight. The scuba buddy support system teaches us to truly rely on one another and to truly look out for one another. Even before we get in the water we engage in a pre-dive safety check where your buddy ensures that your equipment is on properly, and it is their responsibility to turn on your air; your buddy is the one who gives you the very means to survive underwater. You put your life in your buddy's hands.

Sherry's life was in my hands, and when I looked around the boat I couldn't find her. The boat wasn't that big, and Jim was already calling for us to gear up for our second dive. I knew Sherry had been sick too, so I imagined her head would be over the side of the boat somewhere, but I didn't see her. I began to worry. I finally found her at the front of the boat, face down on the floor and very sick.

"Sherry?" No answer. "Sherry, are you OK?"

"No. I am so sick I don't think I can get up and go back in. This is just too much for me. I can't make it."

This woman had supported me for weeks, told me not to quit each week when I wanted to, encouraged me to keep swimming so that we would pass the swim test, and now she was telling me that she was quitting. We had endured months of scuba lessons and swim lessons, embarrassment and triumphs. I was not going to let her throw all of that away because of a tummy ache.

"I'm sick too. Now come on. You got to get up!"

Very slowly she got up and managed to suit up and get back in the water. Once we were under the waves our stomachs stopped churning and we were able to enjoy the beauty of the ocean. We swam around for about forty minutes and saw some incredibly beautiful sights.

When the dive ended and we were about ten feet from the surface I got sick again and brought up the rest of my breakfast. By this time I just accepted the sickness and began looking forward to the next two dives we would do the following day to complete our certification. Sherry and I were going to become certified scuba divers despite our initial inability to swim and our current inability to hold down our food. We would not fail.

The next morning Sherry and I got up, had breakfast, and laughed about our ordeal the day before but admitted how exciting and beautiful it had been underwater. We laughed at ourselves and braced ourselves for another day of waves.

On our way to the boat the captain's wife stopped us. "You two are the most incredible ladies I have ever met. You are some true troopers. After the day you had yesterday, I didn't think I would see you come back."

We admitted that we weren't sure we would be back either, but we were both determined to finish together. We both would have quit weeks ago if it hadn't been for the other, and we were grateful for each other's support.

Our third dive was sixty feet for fifty minutes. The seas were much calmer, and we were able to complete the dive without losing our breakfast. The fourth dive would complete our certification. The dive was thirty-five feet for forty-five minutes at a gorgeous location called The Strip. Once we got to the bottom of the ocean and performed our exercises, Jim made us get into a circle on our knees on the ocean's floor. He had a small plaque in his hand and passed it around to each of us; it read "Congratulations, you are now a PADI-certified Diver." Jim shook each of our hands as he passed the plaque around. We just had a graduation ceremony thirty-five feet below the ocean's surface.

Perhaps the most amazing thing I have ever done in my life, I did on that trip. After we were certified and because we had so many master divers with us on the trip, Jim offered us an incredible opportunity. After all of my tragedies and struggles and uncertainties I did the most incredible thing imaginable. Three months prior, I couldn't swim, and on this day I dove one hundred and thirty feet off the continental shelf. It was the most spectacular feeling and the most spectacular underwater scenery. On that day I knew I had transformed.

SUMMARY

Throughout the course of my story I have been blessed with good support, but oftentimes I suffered from toxic support. Beware of the toxic relationships in your life. The most toxic relationships are often those closest to you, but they will destroy your dreams and your spirit if you let them. The toxic relationships in my life gave me more stress than the situation they were "supporting" me through. Those relationships were draining and required more of me than they offered to me.

I am sure we have all hung on to (or are still hanging on to) a relationship that we know we should have disconnected years ago, but for some reason we feel obligated to stay in the relationship. Much of the problem is often our own codependency; we need to be needed. That's right, we complain about it, but we secretly thrive on the unbalanced friendship. In order to live a healthy life you have to be honest with yourself about what relationships are toxic and which are healthy. Then eliminate the toxic people from your life—friends and family alike.

Recently I was faced with the difficult decision to distance a relationship with a family member because their negative behavior had become more than I could bear. We had been very close for years, and only once did we have a falling out. That disagreement was so severe that we didn't speak for almost two years. When we reconciled I knew I should be cautious about how close I allowed them in my life and was even warned by others in my family to take it slow. Because it was a family member whom I loved and missed, I threw caution to the wind and jumped back into the relationship where we left off.

Nothing had improved about this person's behavior. In fact, it had grown worse and more volatile. I confronted them and begged them to see how their behavior was hurting those they loved. There was no remorse or even recognition that a problem existed, and so with a heavy heart I pulled the plug on the relationship and let it go. I realized that I had been trying to save the relationship because I wanted to fix what was broken in them. Once I made the decision to terminate the relationship I had to stand by my decision.

There are so many people in this story that have shown me positive support and helped me believe in myself when others were content to watch me fail or even convince me to give up. So often the people who were most supportive were the people I knew the least, but they became close friends as we supported each other. Thanks to all the positive people in my life, I have recovered from the emotional scars of losing those dearest to me, I have conquered my fears, and accomplished some amazing achievements. I have become a happier and healthier me, and to date I've lost sixty-five pounds—and I'm still going.

FINAL THOUGHT

WHEN MY EDITOR, Simone Walker, and I finished working on part two of *Hollow*, we discussed what the final thought should be and how we would end the book. I decided we should start where we began—with the answer to the very first question she asked me when we started the editing process. She asked me what I wanted the readers to take away from *Hollow*.

My answer was this: Life will deal you a hand of unfortunate circumstances, but if you continue to play the game the cards will turn in your favor. I love to play Spades, I told Simone, and you don't have to give up and throw in the hand just because you are dealt a hand where it doesn't look like you can make board. Even when you feel like there is no way out of the mess you were dealt, just play out the hand, and most often the cards will turn and you will make your books.

However, let's say you don't make your books and you get set back. Getting set back doesn't mean that the game is over, just that hand. You will get another shot at it when the cards are dealt again. The same concept applies in life. We all have setbacks that will come in the form of death, loss of jobs, or even a down economy. I learned through my life's journey that whenever I am faced with a setback, I always think *comeback*.

Too often in life we tend to give up when things seem difficult.

One of the biggest lessons I learned while writing this book was the fact that I was a great starter of many things but the finisher of none. The old me would give up when there was too much pressure. I knew that in order to complete anything in life, even this book, I had to rely on the strength from God, the wisdom of my mother, the support of family and friends, and the goals and dreams I had set for myself. I knew that I had to stay focused, or I may not even have started the journey toward my dreams and destiny. What helped me most was the fact that I knew many good things had been forecasted in my life, some that had happened and others that were yet to come.

For example, I had dreams of completing this book and owning my own publishing company. I had dreams of helping others fulfill their dreams. I had dreams of traveling the world and seeing places that I had only read about. I had a dream of flying an airplane. If I had quit during the hollowing stage of my life, none of those dreams would ever have happened.

One day while waiting for take-out in one of my favorite restaurants I met a very nice man named Dave Madden. Dave had come to have dinner alone, so he sat at the bar where I was waiting for my dinner. He noticed my phone sitting on the bar and saw a picture of me at a shooting range. When he saw the picture he asked me if that was my weapon and what type of weapon it was. We talked about the shooting range, and he was so fascinated by my story of shooting that he began to ask me what else I liked to do. I told him that I had received my scuba divining certification the year prior and mentioned my deepest dive, one hundred and thirty feet off the Continental Shelf. He was floored by my answer and said he had never met anyone like me.

Then he asked me what I wanted to do next. I told him, after asking him to not laugh at my answer, that I wanted to fly an airplane.

"An airplane?" he asked. "Why do you want to do that?"

I told him that I loved to travel, and I loved to fly. I always wanted to see what the pilot sees when flying a plane. I wanted to be in the midst of the clouds and know what it feels like to fly through them. I told him that I had been through a tough time in my life recently and had experienced the sting of death first-hand. I explained to him, "Once you witness a person talking their last breath, it changes how you see life. I want to live life to the fullest, and it's time for me to begin living out my dreams."

He said, "Wow, you are truly a fascinating woman, and I am taken by your thoughts on life, your goals, and your dreams. Because of that, I am going to bring your dream of flying an airplane to pass."

He told me that he was a pilot who owned his own plane, and he was a flight instructor. One week to the day that I met Dave I took my first flying lesson and logged my first flight hour.

There is a scripture in the Bible in Habakkuk 2:2–3 (AMP) that I was taught a long time ago:

> And the Lord answered me and said, Write the vision and engrave it so plainly upon tablets that everyone who passes may [be able to] read [it easily and quickly] as he hastens by. For the vision is yet for an appointed time and it hastens to the end [fulfillment]; it will not deceive or disappoint. Though it tarry, wait [earnestly] for it, because it will surely come; it will not be behindhand on its appointed day.

I have always loved that scripture and have lived my life knowing that without vision people perish (Prov. 29:18). Had I not known my vision and dreams and been able to articulate them to Dave that day, the dream to fly an airplane may have never come to pass. You see, not only did I write it and post it on my vision board, but I said it aloud. I believe the "everyone who passes" in the above scripture was referring to Dave that day. My vision was so plain that he saw it and was able to underwrite it for me.

So what are you doing or not doing about your dreams? Who

are you sitting next to that might be able to help you underwrite your vision? You have to start dreaming dreams again.
The process of dreaming starts by looking complacency and
resignation in the eye and telling them that they do not have
any influence over you anymore.

I had resigned from so many things in life, and then one day
I discovered that I had resigned from myself. Now, the sky has
no limit for me. If I want it, I go get it. If I dream it, I put the
laws of motion in play. I am my own cause and effect.

No one can steal your dreams, so stop giving them away. It is
time to fall in love with life again instead of just living!

RESOURCES

FOR MORE INFORMATION, consult the following websites:

- The Kübler-Ross Grief Model: *www.wikipedia.org*
- Dorinda Clark-Cole: *www.dorindaclarkcole.net*
- Sweet Potatoes: *www.wikipedia.org*
- Diabetes: *www.diabetes.org*
- Mrs. Dash: *www.mrsdash.com*
- Multiple Sclerosis: *www.nationalmssociety.org*
- *Hollow* and Lynette Jackson: *www.Lynette.TV*
- www.heavenlyseasonings.com

ABOUT THE AUTHOR

LYNETTE JACKSON IS an executive administrative professional with more than fifteen years of experience working with both multimillion-dollar and grassroots community ministries, as well as Fortune 500 companies. She is experienced in:

- Business development

- Client needs assessments

- Market assessment and research

- Productivity improvement

- Strategic business planning

- Strategic sales and marketing

- Product development

- Media/broadcasting development

In 2010 Lynette formed Vision Publishing Group, a publishing company that develops the visions of new authors. She now adds author to her extensive business profile with her newly released book *Hollow: When Everything That Means Anything Is Taken Away*. She is also the winner of *Kontrol* Magazine's 2013 Woman of the Year award, honoring her for her work within the community. She celebrates this accomplishment with her two adult sons, Walter and Ronald, as well as Walter's wife, Shardie, and their son, Christopher.

Lynette is very committed to helping others through her

lifestyle of service and support for multiple sclerosis, lupus, and diabetes research.

CONTACT THE AUTHOR

Website:

www.Lynette.TV